WRITING AND DEFENDING
A THESIS OR DISSERTATION
IN PSYCHOLOGY
AND EDUCATION

WRITING AND DEFENDING
A THESIS OR DISSERTATION
IN PSYCHOLOGY
AND EDUCATION

By

ROY MARTIN, Ph.D

Department of School Psychology
Temple University
Philadelphia, Pennsylvania

HARLES C THOMAS · PUBLISHER

Springfield · Illinois · U.S.A.

Published and Distributed Throughout the World by
CHARLES C THOMAS • PUBLISHER
Bannerstone House
301-327 East Lawrence Avenue, Springfield, Illinois, U.S.A.

© *1980, by* CHARLES C THOMAS • PUBLISHER

ISBN 0-398-03947-X

Library of Congress Catalog Card Number: 79-17283

*With THOMAS BOOKS careful attention is given to all details
of manufacturing and design. It is the Publisher's desire to
present books that are satisfactory as to their physical qualities
and artistic possibilities and appropriate for their particular use.
THOMAS BOOKS will be true to those laws of quality that
assure a good name and good will.*

Printed in the United States of America
WM-6

Library of Congress Cataloging in Publication Data

Martin, Roy, 1943–
    Writing and defending a thesis or dissertation in psychology
and education.

    Bibliography: p.
    Includes index.
    1. Psychological research. 2. Educational research. 3. Psy-
chology—Study and teaching (Graduate) 4. Education—Study
and teaching (Graduate) 5. Dissertations, Academic. I. Title.
BF76.5.M36   150´.7´2   79-17283
ISBN 0-398-03947-X

PREFACE

The thesis and dissertation* are frequently perceived by graduate students in psychology and education as two of the most difficult and anxiety-producing aspects of their course of study. Such feelings result in a large number of persons in these and other fields of study completing all course work for a graduate degree but never receiving the degree because they fail to complete the dissertation.

One reason for these feelings is the number of skills required to successfully carry out a research project. The following is only a partial listing of these skills:

1. Skill in generating a researchable question.
2. Knowledge of and skill in designing research.
3. Skill in obtaining an appropriate and available subject population
4. Knowledge of and skill in the use of various psychological and educational measurement devices.
5. Knowledge of and skill in the use of descriptive and inferential statistical processes.
6. Knowledge of and skill in the use of the computer for carrying out these statistical procedures.
7. Knowledge of and skill in the use of the English language, including grammar and punctuation.

---

*For purposes of simplicity, the term dissertation will be used throughout this discussion to include both master's level and doctoral level terminal research projects.

v

8. Skill in the use of the typewriter.
9. Knowledge of the conventions of one's discipline regarding the format, punctuation, and grammar used in written reports of research.
10. Knowledge of the unwritten conventions regarding the relationship between the graduate student and his/her advisor, between the graduate student and other committee members, and among the committee members, and skill in dealing with these conventions.
11. Knowledge of the conventions of the student's graduate school, college, and department regarding procedures for selecting committees, filing proposals, applying for oral examinations, filing final copies of the thesis or dissertation, etc.

It is rare for a person to feel confident in all the knowledge and skill areas listed. This is particularly true of the graduate student. Furthermore, it is not always clear to whom or to what source the student should go to acquire the information s/he lacks. Finally, the student often feels capable of doing most of the things required for a dissertation if s/he had to do them in isolation, e.g. calculate a statistic, state researchable questions, but there is some concern about being able to put all these pieces together. The student has written reports and papers of various kinds during his/her educational career, but because these reports and papers were of moderate complexity and length, s/he may have developed skills for coping with them that are inappropriate for a task as lengthy and complex as a thesis or dissertation. For example, a bright graduate student may be able to write an acceptable paper in two drafts, writing the first by hand and then typing a final copy from this draft while making minor revisions. When this procedure is attempted on a writing project of some length, it usually results in frustration. For this reason many students need help in breaking down the complex task into a series of small units.

The purpose of this manual is to help a graduate student working on a dissertation to overcome these problems. First, it contains material not usually available in written form. For example, it describes what the student should expect in an oral defense and a framework for understanding the behaviors of the committee members during the oral. Second, it attempts to provide in quickly accessible form information that s/he has been exposed to in the past but which s/he may need some reminder. For example, a discussion of the structure of scientific writing in the social sciences is provided. Finally, an attempt is made to isolate into discrete units the tasks required of the student working on a dissertation and to discuss the most efficient sequencing of these units.

The material presented in this manual is an outgrowth of the experiences of the author as he worked on his own dissertation and as he helped others. Specifically, it attempts to address the questions asked by students in the past eight years, during which time the author has conducted a class entitled "Dissertation Seminar." The opinions expressed are those of the author and may not reflect the opinions of others. The conventions regarding dissertations vary from institution to institution and from program to program, so it would not be possible to report rules that are appropriate in every situation. Furthermore, the material presented is organized around the experience of one instructor in one institution, and the types of problems faced by his students may not be applicable in all cases to those faced by other students. For these reasons, the manual should be used only as a guide, a first step in organizing the student's thinking. The student's advisor and committee are the primary and ultimate sources of information and opinion regarding his/her project.

The student will find this manual most helpful if used in conjunction with a style manual (*Manual for Writers* by Turabian, 1973, or the *Publication Manual* of the American Psychological Association, 1974) and standard texts in research design and statistics. The manual was designed to deal with issues not covered in these sources.

CONTENTS

WRITING AND DEFENDING A THESIS OR DISSERTATION IN PSYCHOLOGY AND EDUCATION

Chapter 1

SELECTING THE RESEARCH TOPIC

One of the most anxiety-producing tasks required in the preparation of a dissertation is simply coming up with a suitable research topic. The anxiety, in part, is generated by the student's realization that in this initial process the stage is being set for the entire project. To a certain extent, the remaining facets of the dissertation are simply an unfolding of the initial idea.

Selecting a research topic is difficult for another reason. Most graduate students are not sure whether the questions that interest them have been addressed by others, whether the questions have been addressed in similar or different forms, or even whether the questions are considered by researchers and/or practitioners in their discipline to be important and worthy of research. This uncertainty is caused by graduate training that is seldom specialized enough to allow the student to understand the frontiers of his/her field. Until the dissertation period, the average student has not had the opportunity to pursue one highly focused area of inquiry for an extended period.

The selection of a research question is one of the most creative aspects of research. Although the creative process remains a mystery, this chapter presents guidelines that may help the student eliminate impediments to the creative process. Specifically, the chapter points out one process a researcher might follow to become acquainted with the cutting edge of an aspect of his/her field. The goal of the chapter is to take the student from the point of having no research topic to the point just prior to preparing a formal research proposal.

PROCESS OF GENERATING A RESEARCH TOPIC

As is often the case in guiding a person through a new process, it is easier to start by saying what not to do in deciding on an area of research than it is to say what steps to follow. Two processes of topic selection that are frequently utilized by the student new to research and that are certain to result in frustration are what the author calls "dreaming in a vacuum" and the "expedient" approach.

Of these two processes, "dreaming in a vacuum" is the most detrimental to research progress. Some students subscribe to the proposition that great research ideas spring forth in a moment of inspiration. The student who subscribes to this notion takes walks in the park, backpacks into remote areas of a favorite mountain retreat, or simply sits in quiet places and waits for inspiration. This strategy, though useful for learning about parks, backpacking, and one's reactions to quiet places, leads to many ABDs (students who have completed all their required work but the dissertation).

The second inappropriate strategy for topic selection is called the "expedient" approach. The exponent of this strategy begins his/her thinking about a topic by first selecting his subject sample, a likeable faculty member as his/her committee chairperson, or even a statistical analysis with which he feels confident, and then by trying to find an idea that fits this situation. This strategy was obviously the plan of choice of a student who approached the author some years back saying that he had access to several years of test results from a psychological clinic and asked if he would help him think of some research that could utilize these data.

Any researcher must have information to think about; s/he must know what other professionals have done in a particular field before s/he can reflect on the importance of any question. The "think-in-a-vacuum strategy" is faulty because it fails to consider that creative thought must be tied to relevant information.

The beginning researcher can obtain information on a given topic from any number of places. The following process seems most efficient. The student should begin with a broad area of inquiry and progressively focus his/her thinking as s/he becomes more sophisticated in that area. This can be done by first looking at texts or summary articles in a topic area, then by reading more specific recent articles in that area. Finally, and this is the step most frequently omitted, the student should spend some time talking to a faculty member with interest and research experience in this area. By doing this, the student will become aware of problems of researching an area that are seldom included in published papers. Another important source of useful information that is often overlooked is past dissertations. This is particularly important when the topic is one that deals with local problems and conditions. Equipped with this background information, the student is in a position to retreat to his/her favorite thinking spot and begin to generate research ideas, to evaluate their theoretical and practical importance, and to consider their importance both professionally and personally.

The difficulties involved in the "expedient" strategy are similar to those involved in the "thinking-in-a-vacuum" strategy. The student may be able to generate questions around a given data pool, but s/he has no frame of reference, no information base with which to select the important questions. The frame of reference is generated only when the student becomes acquainted with the major issues and scholarly opinion in a particular area of research. The student must constantly keep in mind that descriptive statistics can be obtained on any set of numbers whether the numbers have meaning or not. However, research is too expensive and time consuming to allow all possible relationships between data bits to be examined. The limited time and energies of the researcher must be focused on those questions that have the most promise of making an important difference, theoretically and practically.

Often-overlooked Sources of Ideas

One of the most useful sources of information regarding research trends in a particular psychological or educational area are the reference works and journals that review research. The following is a brief annotated bibliography of a few of the most important sources of this type:

1. *The American Psychologist*

This journal is published monthly by the American Psychological Association and is sent to all members of the association. The articles selected by the editors are of broad psychological interest and often take review form. Once annually, all the articles of that year are listed in an index enclosed in the December issue.

2. *Annual Review of Psychology*

Each yearly volume of the *Annual Review* contains highly comprehensive and integrated reviews of about twenty research areas in psychology. Some topics are reviewed often (almost every year) while others are reviewed perhaps every five years. The user should look over the six or seven most recent volumes to get an idea of coverage.

3. *Handbook of Research on Teaching*

Published by the American Educational Research Association, this handbook provides highly comprehensive reviews of educational research. Two volumes have been published to date, the last one in 1973.

4. *Harvard Educational Review*

Edited and published by graduate students at Harvard University, this journal provides reviews and opinions on the most topical educational issues.

5. *Review of Educational Research*

Published by the American Educational Research Association, this quarterly journal publishes review articles which summarize, in a comprehensive and integrated fashion, research on educational topics.

6. *Yearbook of the National Society for the Study of Education (NSSE)*

Since 1902, the Yearbook has published an annual volume organized around some central theme, e.g. Behavior Modification in Education. The articles are then written by distinguished scholars in these areas. The topics are selected because of their timeliness or immediate practical value to educators and researchers.

CRITERIA FOR TOPIC SELECTION

Up to this point it has been implied that the student's interest is the primary criterion for topic selection. However, there are several other considerations that must be kept in mind in topic selection. First, the topic should be related to the student's field of study. Bright graduate students read in areas of interest not closely related to their predominant field of study and are sometimes tempted to research these areas. Although one hesitates to frustrate a creative impulse, dissertation research outside one's area of training can lead to difficulty. Breaking into a new research area often creates a feeling of excitement that the old familiar area does not. However, as one becomes more acquainted with the new one, the novelty usually wears off and the problems and difficulties of researching that area begin to be understood. Furthermore, if a dissertation topic is far removed from the student's major area of training, there may be no faculty member available in the department who has interest and experience in that line of inquiry. Some departments have written or unwritten rules that discourage having a major advisor outside one's academic specialty. Doing this tends to be viewed as a sign of professional identity confusion. There is another problem with choosing a topic unrelated to one's area of training—it creates confusion on the part of prospective employers about the student's professional identity and area of interest.

On the other hand, there is a strong tendency within the academic world to allow faculty and students to follow their interests no matter where they may lead. Thus, a good deal of latitude is allowed in selecting topics that are not part of the mainstream of the person's discipline or profession. The graduate student working on a dissertation will avoid difficulty if s/he can in some way relate the topic to the content focus of the department. For example, a special education student trained to teach the blind might be interested in the issue of longitudinal stability of IQ or in the effects of a mother's working during her child's preschool years on the child's academic achievement in the first grade. If these topics can be related to other areas, often the best interests of the students will have been served.

Another major criterion against which a topic should be judged is its practicality. The average master's student, because of educational and employment constraints, allows from four to nine months for his/her thesis, and a doctoral student may allow from nine to eighteen months. Furthermore, most thesis and dissertation research is not funded, so the student incurs all the expenses of the project. These time and financial constraints greatly limit the scope of the research a student can undertake.

There is a tendency, on the student's part, when planning a major task like a dissertation to feel that it can be completed more quickly than is realistic. This miscalculation results from the idea that everything will go as planned, that there will be no unforeseen contingencies. As any construction contractor or experienced researcher knows, this is rarely the case. A good rule of thumb is to plan for a dissertation or thesis to take from one-fourth to one-third more time than originally expected.

Sometimes students commit themselves to projects that are difficult to carry out because they feel that they have devoted too much time to a topic to begin a new one. Perhaps they have already prepared a literature review and do not want to waste the time already spent. In most cases, however, the time spent in preparing a review or even a complete formal proposal is only a fraction of the time it takes to collect data under diffcult circumstances or to build exotic apparatuses or measurement devices. An acquaintance of the author's became committed to just such a dissertation topic, one that required commuting 200 miles to get a handful of data. Due to subject absences, administrative pitfalls, and other time commitments, the dissertation was extended one year beyond the student's expected completion date. In addition, he had to purchase a new car sooner than was planned due to the extended amount of driving required by data collection.

The student should not rely on faculty advisors to protect him/her from becoming involved in projects that are too difficult to handle. Their interest in the project's outcome may be great enough to dull their sense of responsibility about getting the student to the graduation ceremony as soon as possible.

Another major criterion, already alluded to, for evaluating a thesis or dissertation idea deserves further emphasis: dissertation topics should utilize the interest and expertise of one or more of the student's faculty advisors. No researcher works entirely alone, although his/her name may be the only one on the project. As pointed out in the Preface to this manual, there are too many different tasks required in research projects for one person to skillfully accomplish them without at least some consultation from other knowledgeable persons. Leaving methodological (design, statistics, etc.) and production (writing, typing reproduction, etc.) skills aside, few researchers feel they know so much about one content area that they need not seek help from others to clarify their thoughts.

Consultation is important for the mature researcher, but it is more important for the student researcher because of his/her lack of experience. Understanding the timely and important questions in an area of inquiry requires historical perspective that few students can be expected to have. Much important information regarding measurement problems and procedural pitfalls is not discussed in research writing and must be obtained firsthand from those with experience. Thus, even a brilliant idea has little chance of resulting in important and personally satisfying research unless at least one member of a student's committee can offer substantive support.

The Originality Issue

Many students, as they begin to think about a research topic, are concerned that a dissertation must be original and that someone else has done exactly the same project they are planning. In one sense this is a false issue, for no research is original. All research is based on the work of others, on their measurement techniques and their procedures. In fact, the most useful kind of research is that which is based very closely on previous work and seeks to clarify an uncertain point by varying only one detail of the methodology.

From another point of view, it is nearly impossible to do research that is not original. A replication, in which a methodology is exactly duplicated, is seldom done on exactly the same subjects, although it may be done on subjects with characteristics similar to those of the first study. Even if it were done on the same subjects, time would have passed since the earlier measurements were taken so that these subjects would now be different in some ways.

Some academic departments might frown on several students using the same methodology on subjects with similar characteristics due to a feeling that the student should have the experience of devising his/her own methodology. The author's position would be that a sound scientific problem on which several students wanted to work with very similar methodologies might be a fine way to accumulate knowledge and also develop an understanding of research procedure.

In any event, originality should not be considered in the beginning phases of topic selection. Afterwards, as the idea becomes progressively more focused, originality may cease to be an issue, since the focusing of the topic is based on a progressively more thorough understanding of what has been done in an area and what needs to be done.

THE FIRST PROPOSAL DRAFT

Assuming that the student has isolated an area of research through reading and conversation with others, s/he now comes to the stage of making some preliminary decisions. These decisions involve the composition of the subject sample and the selection of measurement devices, an experimental procedure, a research design, and an analysis schema. These topics have probably been discussed with others during the topic selection stage, and perhaps some preliminary decisions on major methodological aspects of the research project have been made. It is now time to complete this preliminary phase of planning and write down the resulting decisions. The purposes of these notes are threefold:

1. To further clarify the procedure and to force consideration of those aspects of the project that may have been previously overlooked.
2. To provide a brief document that a prospective advisor can look over and comment upon.
3. To provide a document that explains the experimental procedures so that tentative approval for access to a subject population can be obtained.

This rough draft serves another important purpose, although it is somewhat less tangible than those just mentioned. For the student who approaches writing the dissertation with anxiety, who does not feel s/he could ever write 100 to 200 pages on any topic, this first draft provides a successful writing experience. Because of its brevity, this draft can usually be handled without great effort or anxiety. Furthermore, it provides an example of the process that will be followed on the entire project — that is, breaking the complex task down into small, accomplishable units. With this rough draft complete, the student realizes that the remaining steps in finishing the project are simply an expansion of this outline. This realization may demystify the writing task somewhat.

The document should be structured as follows:

1. Statement of the problem or rationale of the study

2. Statement of the purpose of the study
3. Listing of the research questions
4. Definition of terms
5. Subjects, characteristics, number, and selection procedure
6. Description of design
7. Description of measurement devices and other material
8. Description of procedure
9. Description of data analysis

This first draft should be brief. The review of literature incorporated in the statement of the problem or rationale section should include only the two or three most important sources or studies that guided the researcher. The hypotheses should be stated in directional form. (Most researchers feel that the statement of the null hypotheses is archaic even in the final copy of the dissertation.) The definition of terms section should be omitted unless the hypotheses cannot be understood without its inclusion. Subjects, materials, and procedure should be discussed in some detail.

It has been the author's experience that the entire draft should not exceed six or seven pages in length. If the student writes a detailed proposal and has spent a good deal of time refinishing each aspect of the project, s/he will have become so ego involved in it that s/he will resist, or selectively perceive, the opinions offered by others. This is a preliminary draft, not a finished product. Its purpose is to provide an efficient means by which the student can seek clarification of major ideas and pick up errors while it is easy to do so. If the student is the kind who always writes longer papers than his/her peers, s/he sould resist the temptation in this case. The chance to demonstrate verbal virtuosity will come.

MAKING INITIAL CONTACT WITH THE MAJOR ADVISOR

The last stage of topic selection is to obtain preliminary approval for the broad outlines of the proposed project. The first person from whom approval should be obtained is a faculty member who might serve as a thesis or dissertation advisor. The student should present the first draft of the proposal to the chosen faculty member and seek his/her opinion on all the major aspects of the proposed project. If there is some level of agreement that the basic ideas presented are sound, the student might approach the subject of whether or not this person would consider being his/her major advisor. The faculty member's opinion regarding others who could serve on the committee might also be sought.

Often the question of chairmanship or membership on the committee will be contingent upon an acceptable formal proposal. In fact, with the exception of the chairperson, the other committee persons may not wish to discuss their membership until a formal proposal has been prepared. In most graduate institutions the mechanism for formally indicating acceptance of a committee position is the faculty member's signature on the cover of the formal proposal.

In some departments, in order to expedite the student's progress in preparing a formal proposal, one faculty member is given the responsibility for working with students as they select their topics and begin to prepare their proposals. Sometimes this function is served in the context of an independent study or in a course entitled "Dissertation Seminar" or "Research Practicum." Under this system, the rough proposal is submitted to the instructor and is judged in terms of general feasibility and appropriateness of the methodology. Prospective committee members are usually not approached until a formal proposal has been prepared.

OBTAINING ACCESS TO SUBJECT POPULATION AND MATERIALS

In addition to obtaining tentative approval of his/her research idea from a prospective committee chairperson, the student should also get approval for access to an appropriate subject population. In coming to some agreement with the person in charge of the subject population, the short proposal described previously is very helpful. It is often preferable to the formal, extended proposal because the responsible parties are busy people and need only to understand the major aspects of the study and the requirements of the subjects to make their decision.

One of the more difficult aspects of obtaining tentative approval on the subject population is determining whose prerogative it is to give this permission. For example, if the researcher plans to use students attending public or private schools, is permission sought from classroom teachers, principals, superintendents, boards of education, or a research committee? It has been the author's experience that the classroom teacher's permission, although necessary, is seldom sufficient. At minimum, the principal's sanction is necessary. In some school systems the permission of these two parties is all that is required. But in schools that are proximate to universities or for other reasons are the focus of considerable research attention, there is usually a more involved approval procedure. This may include appearances before the board of education or a research committee and the presentation of letters of recommendation, a formal proposal, and documents discussing legal liability.

In addition to the various procedural requirements of the institutional representatives, the researcher should begin to consider the question of subject permission or parental permission in the case of minors. Few types of research do not require written permission on the part of subjects or their guardians. So, the student should explore the institution's policies regarding this matter, ask the opinion of his faculty advisor, and consult the American Psychological Association (APA) guide for ethical use of human subjects. Furthermore, the institution should be approached to determine its policy regarding the mechanics of obtaining parental or subject permission, e.g. will they send out letters on their stationery endorsing the project, or will the researcher carry out this function unaided?

Finally, the researcher may wish to use measurement devices or other kinds of apparatus that are not available except from the developer. In such cases, as soon as the research idea is crystalized, permission to use such materials should be sought, and made regarding purchase or rental fees.

SUMMARY

1. Do not wait for inspiration or try to generate a researchable topic without studying a topic area first.

2. Do not select a topic solely because a congenial faculty member is interested in it, because there is an available subject population, or because a related question can be analyzed using a familiar statistical procedure.
3. Do read texts, reviews of recent research, and recent journal articles that cover the proposed field of inquiry. Talk with faculty members who have interest and experience in this type of research.
4. Pick a project that can be accomplished within a reasonable time limit.
5. Pick a project topic that can be related to the major field of study.
6. Pick a project topic in which one or more faculty members have expertise and interest.
7. Write a brief proposal emphasizing methodological and rationale issues as soon as the idea begins to crystalize.
8. Seek the approval of a tentative project advisor for the major aspects of the study.
9. Make initial contact regarding subject populations and accessibility to materials as soon after the idea has crystalized as possible.

Chapter 2

THE FORMAL PROPOSAL AND THE COMMITTEE SELECTION

The student has committed himself/herself to an area of research and has written a brief proposal that presents the major facets of the project. S/he has also found a faculty member who has expressed both tentative approval of the project and an interest in serving as the chairperson of the committee. At this point, two major steps must be completed before the student can begin to carry out the project. S/he must write a formal research proposal. Then s/he must present the proposal to selected faculty members for their approval. The faculty members selected for this task will usually become his/her committee upon approving the proposal. The purpose of this chapter is to provide some guidelines for the preparation of the formal proposal and the selection of a committee.

FORMAT OF THE FORMAL PROPOSAL

Two general approaches can be taken to the organization of the formal research proposal. One approach, referred to here as Format A, is similar to the rough draft format suggested in Chapter 1, with the addition of a review of the literature and a time line section. The second approach, referred to as Format B, organizes the proposal in the same way as the first three chapters of the thesis or dissertation.

19

Format A

The following presents the headings of Format A:

Problem or Rationale
Purpose
Hypotheses
Definition of Terms
Review of Literature
Subjects
Design
Materials
Procedure
Data Analysis Procedures
Proposed Time Line

The problem section presents questions that the researcher seeks to answer with his/her project and discusses the importance of these questions. The problem statement itself is usually in question form, showing the relationship of two or more variables. An example of a problem statement is the following: Does a teacher's knowledge of the IQ of his/her students affect the teacher's classroom interactions with those students? One variable is knowledge of IQ of students, and the other is classroom interaction. The verb *affect* of course, indicates the relationship—in this case a cause-effect relationship. The discussion of the importance of the problem should be relatively brief, citing only the most important sources. (For a more extended discussion of the Problem section see Chapter 3, Introduction.)

The Purpose section is usually quite brief. It points out in a few sentences the aspect of the problem on which the researcher plans to focus. In the previously cited example, the procedure for creating teacher knowledge of student IQ, the types of classroom interaction that will be measured, and the nature of the control or comparison group have not been discussed. In other words, in its present form the research question is untestable. The purpose, then, briefly tells the reader how the researcher will deal with the question. The sample purpose might read as follows:

The purpose of the present study is to eliminate the methodological weaknesses discussed by Smith and Jones (1970) by having the teacher serve as her own control. Each teacher will be made aware of the IQs of students in three sections of her English class but will not be given the IQs of students in the other three sections. Furthermore, the effects of this knowledge on three types of child-initiated responses will be tested in addition to the three types of teacher-initiated responses reported by Smith and Jones.

The Hypothesis section presents the research hypothesis. Most researchers feel presenting the statistical or null hypotheses is unnecessary, although some members of a committee may wish to see them included. The research hypotheses should, of course, state the researcher's expectations about the relationship between the variables; these should be stated in operational or testable form. The following is a testable hypothesis:

Students with high IQs (as measured by the Stanford Binet) in the classes where the teacher knows their IQs will have more student-initiated procedural contacts (as measured through direct observation) than high IQ students in the classes in which the teacher does not know their IQs.

The Definition of Terms section follows the purpose and Hypotheses sections and serves to define the terms used in these sections that might be unfamiliar to the reader or ambiguous in the present context. The Definition of Terms section may not always be necessary if all the concepts and variables are familiar ones. In the above example, *IQ* would not need to be defined. However, if the researcher feels there is any doubt about the reader's clear understanding of the terms, they should be defined. Continuing the example, the following are two of several terms that would require definitions:

Classroom interaction — Classroom interaction is limited to six types of dyadic interactions between a teacher and a student. The term as it is used here explicitly excludes interactions between the teacher and the entire class or a group of students.

Child-initiated procedural contacts — Procedural contacts are teacher-student contacts in which the child asks to pass out papers, go to the bathroom, or do some other activity distinct from asking for help with academic work.

The contents of the Review of Literature, Subjects, Design, Materials, and Procedure sections of the proposal are very similar to the corresponding sections in the dissertation. Since these sections are discussed in detail in Chapter 3, they will not be discussed here.

The Data Analysis section of the proposal discusses the data reduction procedures and the decision rules that will be used in testing the hypotheses. This section of the proposal is the one usually given the least attention by the student. It is not, for example, sufficient to say that the hypotheses will be tested by a series of oneway analyses of variance.

This does not tell the reader what kind of descriptive statistics will be used. The student has not indicated whether or not s/he will test the assumptions of the inferential statistics he plans to use, or if he plans to use *post hoc* tests if a significant *F* is obtained. What level of significance is the researcher using? What computation program does s/he plan to use? All these question should be addressed in the proposal. In addition, the student may find it helpful to produce a set of blank tables showing how s/he plans to present the data in the dissertation.

In summary, the student should resist the temptation to avoid the data analysis questions until the data is in hand. This is especially true for the student who is a little anxious about the statistical aspects of research. Advanced planning will help avoid wasted effort and anxiety.

The final section of the proposal, the Time Line, is not always required but is helpful to the student and the committee. It consists of the student's indicating on what dates s/he proposes to have completed each phase of the project. A typical time line might include an indication of the date the student expects to have the proposal approved, the date that the data collection is expected to be completed, the date the analysis will be complete, the date of the first complete draft of the dissertation, and finally, the date of the final oral examination. This proposed time line is in no way a commitment to the committee. It simply gives the committee an indication of the student's plans. It is useful in that the committee may be able to adjust the student's expectations to make them more realistic or point out ways to reduce the time necessary to complete a given phase.

Format B

Format B addresses the same points as Format A but organizes them in a different manner and thus utilizes different headings. Format B is written in the manner of the first three chapters of the dissertation with the exception that the methodology section and other sections are written in the future tense where necessary.

Format B has the following structure (for a detailed discussion see Chapter 3):

Introduction
Review of Literature
Method
Data Analysis Procedures
Time Line

The Introduction includes the problem and purpose statements and sometimes the hypotheses. If the hypotheses are not located in the Introduction, they are usually located at the end of the Review of Literature section. The Method section includes a discussion of the subjects, design, materials, and procedures, each of which are treated as a subsection and given a subheading. The Data Analysis and Time Line sections are organized in the same manner as in Format A.

One major difference between Formats A and B is cosmetic—that is, it involves a restructuring of the headings. Another difference is that Format B requires a more thorough integration of the material discussed than is required by Format A, particularly in the Introduction section. Finally, these formats differ in the emphasis given the Review of Literature. The standard proposal does not require as comprehensive a review as would be expected in the final manuscript of the dissertation. However,

some students feel that if they are becoming involved in the literature review, they should carry it
to completion. Format B, then, typically is used by
students who want to write a review that will serve
as a first draft of the review chapter of their dissertation. The only change that will need to be made
at the time of writing the final manuscript is to include articles that have been published between the
time of the writing of the proposal and the time of
the final manuscript.

Both proposal structures have advantages and
disadvantages. The advantages of Format A are
that it briefly communicates all the necessary information a committee needs to judge the value of the
project. It also presents this information in an easily
identifiable form, since each topic is identified by a
heading. The advantage of Format B is that it requires the student to make a first draft of the first
three chapters of the dissertation and if approved,
it gives him/her a headstart on writing the final
manuscript. Many committee members, however,
want to separate the two tasks of deciding on the
appropriateness of a project and dealing with the
manner in which it is written. If the committee does
not want to help with the organization and integration of the written product at the proposal stage,
then Format B is inappropriate. Thus the choice
between these formats should be worked out with
the committee, and the choice depends on the
customs of the institution, the time available to
committee members at different stages of the dissertation process, and the manner in which the
chairperson prefers to work.

In addition to the proposal structure, the student
should seek the committee's opinion as to the style

in which the proposal should be written. The choice is usually between the style dictated by the American Psychological Association's *Publication Manual* (1974) and the style suggested by Turabian in *A Manual for Writers* (1973). Both manuals cover such topics as how footnotes are dealt with, how references are made, etc.

CONDUCTING A COMPUTERIZED LITERATURE SEARCH

One of the ways in which the draft proposal is developed into a formal proposal is by expanding the Literature section of the draft. Formerly, doctoral or master's students working on a research project had to do their literature search by hand. In the past few years, however, universities, educational resource centers, and private companies have developed the capability to do computerized literature searches. These searches can augment the literature review the student would do by himself/herself.

Some students working on a dissertation seem to feel that such searches are cheating or that their committees will frown upon a review compiled in this way. A computer literature search, however, should be looked at in the same light as the use of the computer for statistical operations. That is, the computer simply allows the researcher to do routine clerical tasks much faster and more accurately than s/he could do unassisted.

The student should understand also that a computer literature search does not eliminate the necessity for substantial library work. This is true because the data presented to the user of a computerized literature search is only a reference or a reference plus a brief abstract of the materials selected. If the referenced material is of interest to the researcher, s/he must read it in the original source. Thus a computer search only helps the user locate important material. Also, no matter how well search descriptors are written (the key words the computer uses to decide which article to print), important material will be overlooked. Some important material will appear in journals that are not referenced in the data bases the computer scans. The user may also not scan all the appropriate data bases. Furthermore data bases typically do not cover older material and cannot remain absolutely current. (For example, *Psychological Abstracts* only extends from the year 1967 to the present.) For all these reasons no computer search will be complete. Finally, the researcher may want to see what has happened in the literature between the time of writing the proposal and the time of writing the final report, and since computer searches are expensive, s/he may have to cover the most recent material through library research.

The most frequently used computer systems are the System Development Corporation (SDC) and the Lockheed Corporation (DIALOG) systems. A student interested in using these systems and other systems like them locates a terminal that is connected to these systems (usually at a university library or a regional educational resource center). With help at the terminal site, the user communicates with the computer via a telephone hookup. His/her output comes in the form of on-line printouts, which are obtained immediately at the remote site, or in the form of off-line printouts, which are printed at the computer site and shipped to the user. The off-line system is significantly less expensive than the on-line system. In any case the cost of such a search ranges from about five to one hundred dollars, depending on the number of citations printed and the location of the printing.

The user of these systems has the option of selecting from a series of data bases those that s/he feels will be most likely to uncover important information. The data bases of most interest to educators and psychologists are the following:

1. ERIC—Information from the ERIC reports and from the current *Index of Journals in Education* (1966 to present).
2. *Exceptional Child Education Abstracts*—Information from the Council of Exceptional Children (1969 to present).
3. AIM/ARM—Instructional and research material from the Center for Vocational and Technical Education (1967 to present).
4. *Dissertation Abstracts*—All American dissertations collected by University Microfilms (1861 to present).
5. *Psychological Abstracts*—References to material in APA journals by the American Psychological Association (1967 to present).
6. *Social Scisearch*—Social science references from The Institute for Scientific Information (ISI) (1972 to present).

The typical computerized literature search is carried out by the use of descriptor words. In this type of search, the researcher writes the specific question s/he is interested in, then picks out the main terms of this question. For example, the question might be, What is the attitude of blacks toward mental health programs in secondary schools? If the ERIC data base was being scanned, the user would pick out three types of terms: a subject term, a target term, and a leveling term. In the example used here, the subject term is "attitudes toward mental health programs" because it is the major concern of the documents of interest. The target term indicates the group of persons in question, in this case "blacks." The leveling term is the specific grade or educational level of concern, in this case "secondary schools." When these terms have been isolated, they are then located in a master list of descriptor terms. Another list of terms is available that will show how many articles or documents one can expect from a single descriptor or a combination of descriptors.

With the help of a computer specialist or a search specialist, the researcher draws up a search strategy. The descriptors are grouped and manipulated by "and/or" logical statements—for example: A plus (B plus C), or (A or B) plus C. The latter statement might indicate that the user wanted to access all articles referenced that related to attitudes toward mental health (A) or attitudes toward health (B) if they also related to attitudes of blacks (C).

For the researcher interested in the most current information in a given area of research, an important source is the Smithsonian Science Information Exchange (SSIE). This exchange prepares literature searches of funded research in progress, obtaining its information from 1,300 supporting organizations, including granting agencies of the federal, state, and local governments, foundations, nonprofit associations, and universities. The SSIE conducts custom searches using key descriptor terms as well as packaged searches. The latter is a current listing of all research being carried out in a specific field such as hyperkinetic children, or autistic, schizophrenic, or psychotic children. Such packages range in cost from forty to sixty dollars. Although designed for those planning to apply for grants, this kind of computerized search may be helpful to some dissertation students, especially if they are interested in an area in which major research efforts are currently underway.

TYPING THE PROPOSAL

Although graduate schools or departments usually have no formal guidelines regarding the production of the proposal, the following general typing regulations should be followed:

1. A one-and- one-half-inch margin at left and top; a one-inch margin at the other sides.
2. Pages should be numbered at the top right-hand corner, one inch down and one inch from the right edge of the paper . No page number is required on the first page.
3. Double space the entire proposal, including the reference section. This allows the committee and others reading the proposal to write corrections or editorial comments between typed lines. Triple space after a title or centered heading.
4. The proposal can be typed on ordinary typing paper. It need not be sulfite or cotton bond. However, erasable bond should not be used.
5. The student should make at least six copies of the original proposal when it is approved — one copy for each committee member (usually three), one that is usually filed with the grad-

uate school or department, and two for himself.

These suggestions should be followed only if the committee or university regulations do not dictate specific criteria. The student may wish to consult the APA *Publication Manual* (1974) or the Turabian *Manual for Writers* (1973) for additional style considerations.

COMMITTEE SELECTION

Most colleges and universities have specific guidelines regarding the size and composition of thesis and dissertation committees. Typically, committees consist of three persons, one of whom is designated as a chairperson. Some universities require that at least one of the committee persons be from a department other than the student's major department. In some universities the committee may be made up entirely of members outside the student's department, while in others at least the chairperson must be a member of the student's major department. In some cases committee persons need not even be on the faculty of the university in which the student is enrolled.

Practical Considerations in Committee Selection

The student should choose his/her committee with care. At least four factors should be considered in this deliberation. First, the committee member must be someone with whom the student can work. In particular, the student should resist the temptation to select a committee member on the basis of scholarly reputation if in the past they have had difficulty relating to one another.

A second factor to consider is the time availability of the prospective committee member. Again, a nationally known scholar may be a poor choice because of his/her commitments to his/her own research activity. Others for whom time availability may be a problem are department chairpersons, persons who are very active in local, state, or national professional organizations, or persons who are already on a number of dissertation committees.

The interest of the faculty member in the student's topic is another important consideration, and perhaps it is more important than his/her time availability. If a faculty member is truly interested in a particular topic, s/he will usually find the time to help a student investigate that topic. The error most often made by the student in this regard is to select one member who is a methodologist with the idea that this person will be helpful with questions about the design and statistical analysis. Unless the methodological questions are particularly involved or the methodologist is interested in the content of the dissertation, this is a waste of time. Most faculty members who do research have methodological skills that are strong enough to help the student, and in special problem areas a brief conference with a methodologist may be all that is required. Unless the project is designed to answer methodological questions, the student should confine his/her choices to persons interested in the content area of the project.

The final criterion for committee selection is that the committee members themselves must be able to get along. The particular problem encountered here usually involves authority problems between the chairperson and another committee member. The chairperson is generally acknowledged as having the final word in decisions regarding differences of opinion among committee members, but this power is rarely used, since there is also a strong tendency on such committees toward negotiation and compromise. This process breaks down when one committee member is clearly more expert in the topic area of the student's research than the chairperson and when the chairperson does not acknowledge this in making decisions. The process can also break down in cases where two "experts" with different approaches to a problem, e.g. persons having different theoretical orientations, are on the same committee. To avoid this problem, the student should choose as the committee chairperson the faculty member with the most interest and expertise in the area of the proposed research and ask for suggestions from this chairperson when selecting other members. Often faculty members are reluctant to acknowledge that they have trouble working with another faculty member once a committee has been formed; to avoid embarrassment or problems within a committee, it is prudent for the student not to select the committee before speaking with the chairperson.

TACTICS IN WORKING WITH THE COMMITTEE

Two general procedures are followed in obtaining approval of a dissertation proposal. The procedure followed depends on how the chairperson of the committee perceives his/her role. Some chairpersons prefer to do most of the work in criticizing or making alterations in the proposal, with the remainder of the committee reading the proposal only after it has been tentatively approved by the chairperson. The advantage of this system is that it tends to build a strong working relationship between the chairperson and the student, and it may be more efficient for the student to deal with one person rather than three early in the proposal-writing process. The disadvantage is that it fosters a lack of involvement by the other committee members in the project. They then may rely too heavily on the chairperson to work with the student. Also, the other committee members may be reluctant to criticize the proposal when it has been approved by the chairperson because they fear such criticism will be seen as criticism of the chairperson.

The alternate procedure is to submit drafts of the proposal to all committee members simultaneously and adjust the proposal to fit the demands of all three committee members at one time. This process keeps the committee members involved in careful and active reading of the drafts. However, it may be an inefficient process for the members in that all of them must comment on obvious writing, methodological, or reasoning errors. In effect, the same editorial work is done three times. Also, it may be more difficult for the student to get speedy responses on proposal drafts from three persons than from one.

The decision about which tactic to use should be left to the chairperson, because this person will know how s/he works best and may know what the other committee members expect. When the chairperson has stated his/her preference, the student should notify and seek the approval of the other committee members for this procedure.

Despite careful committee selection, committee members occasionally have diametrically opposing views with regard to an issue. Instead of seeing individual members, trying to satisfy each one in succession, the student should press for a full committee meeting on the subject so that quick closure can be obtained. In face-to-face discussion, the members often come to a compromise. If they cannot agree, this should be determined as soon as possible so that arrangements can be made to replace one of the conflicting members.

The student, pressed by time deadlines, often feels that if s/he communicates to the committee members the importance of his/her deadlines, they will read the proposal more quickly. When the faculty member does not respond quickly, the student feels the faculty member is being insensitive to his/her needs. The student usually forgets in this situation that it has taken him/her two months to one year to write the proposal because other activities in his/her life have taken a higher priority than the proposal. Faculty members are busy people, most holding teaching, research, and university service commitments in a delicate balance. They resent impassioned pleas for speed in reading proposals.

A rule of thumb is to allow two weeks for a faculty member to respond to a proposal draft. If that much time has passed, the student has the right to seek clarification regarding when a response will be forthcoming. In cases of real negligence, the student should not hesitate to seek a new committee member. This usually occurs when a faculty member finds that his/her research activity or university service has become overwhelming, and s/he may welcome being relieved of the committee obligation. Such a step should be taken only in consultation with the committee chairperson and only after a face-to-face meeting with the offending faculty member has taken place. Departments in graduate schools may have procedural rules that must be followed in order to reconstitute a committee.

SUMMARY

1. The formal proposal may be written in modified outline form or in a prose format similar to that of the first three chapters of the dissertation. Check with the committee for an indication of its preference.

2. The dissertation can be written in a number of styles, but usually the suggestions of Turabian or the APA *Publication Manual* are followed. Check with the committee for an indication of its preference.

3. Data analysis procedures should be given as thorough a treatment in the proposal as other methodological aspects, i.e. they should be spelled out in detail.

4. The student should strongly consider utilizing a computerized literature search procedure to aid in developing his/her review of the literature.

5. The proposal is typed on plain typing paper (not erasable bond), with one- and- one-half inch margins on the top and left and one inch margins elsewhere. The entire proposal should be double spaced and numbered at the top right-hand corner.

6. The student should check on department or university regulations regarding the number

and departmental affiliation of committee members.

7. Committee persons should be chosen who have time to serve, have an interest in the proposed research topic, and can work with the candidate and one another.

8. In general, the student should ask the person who has the most expertise in the area of his/her research to be the chairperson.

9. The student should discuss with his/her chairperson the procedure to be used in seeking committee feedback on the proposal.

References

American Psychological Association. *Publication manual* (2nd ed.). Washington, D. C.: American Psychological Association, 1974.

Turabian, K. L. *A manual for writers* (4th ed.). Chicago: University of Chicago Press, 1973.

Chapter 3

THE STRUCTURE OF THESES AND DISSERTATIONS

Probably no other aspect of writing so quickly distinguishes between the professional and the amateur writer than the emphasis on structure. The student writer, for example, frequently starts writing at the beginning of Chapter 1 of a dissertation with the hope of working his/her way to the end of the chapter with little more in mind regarding structure than the three or four most important points. Such a neglect of structure is the primary cause of the situation most feared by all writers — sitting for an hour in front of a blank sheet of paper trying to compose the first sentence.

The purpose of this chapter is to point out the framework around which an empirical investigation is written. The writer of empirical reports in psychology and education is fortunate in that one structure is almost universally utilized in these disciplines. The principal components of the structure are the chapters of the dissertation and the corresponding sections of the journal article. These typically are the Introduction, the Review of Literature, the Method, the Results, and the Discussion. The primary difference between the journal article and the dissertation is that in the journal article the review of the literature is omitted or incorporated in a brief form in the introduction.

Most graduate students have read journal articles in their disciplines and are aware of this basic structure. It is the internal organization of each chapter or section that is often less well understood. This chapter is devoted to a discussion of the internal structure of each chapter of a dissertation or section of a journal article.

THE INTRODUCTION

The purpose of the introduction is to provide the rationale for the investigation, an overview of the processes that are going to be used in the investigation, and the questions that the investigation is designed to answer. One section of the introduction is devoted to each of these functions, and the sections are usually referred to as the Problem, the Purpose, and the Hypotheses sections.

An educator and psychologist spends his/her time doing research because there is a problem s/he cannot solve or a question s/he cannot answer. Such problems involve a lack of clear or complete information in his/her discipline. More specifically, the problem usually arises out of four circumstances:

1. There is little or no research on a particular topic. An example of such a topic would be, What processes should a consulting psychologist use to insure that his/her recommendation to educators will be seriously considered or followed?

2. There is some research, but it has not been applied to enough samples or in enough situations to be considered a reliable phenomenon. Stated another way, the limits of the extent to which the phenomenon can be generalized are unknown. During the 1960's, for example, much of the research in behavior modification was designed to demonstrate that this

technology could be successfully applied to groups other than institutionalized retarded or emotionally disturbed persons.

3. There is a good deal of research, but the findings are contradictory. This kind of problem has occurred in the research on the effects of adult praise and reproof on the behavior of children.

4. There are two theories that explain the same phenomena but that recommend or predict different outcomes of a common action, and the researcher is concerned about which theoretical orientation to follow. For example, psychoanalytic theory recommends acting out one's aggressions in limited ways based on the concepts of catharsis. Learning theories do not recommend acting out aggressive impulses on the grounds that by doing so even in a limited way, the behavior pattern of aggression will be strengthened and perhaps generalized to inappropriate circumstances.

In building the case for one of the above types of problems, the researcher is also required to give the reader an idea why the problem is of importance. Simply because there is little research in an area does not make the area worthy of investigation. The writer must build a case that indicates that the problem is worthy of the time and effort required to solve it.

The delineation of the problem leads directly to the statement of the purpose. The purpose of any study is to help solve the stated problem. This subsection is designed to give the reader a brief overview of how the researcher plans to answer the questions or problems already mentioned. To illustrate this, if the problem were that there was little research on the factors that relate to school achievement in rural southern school districts, then the purpose would be to help remedy that problem by conducting an exploratory study using variables that have been found to correlate with achievement in other populations. A general description of the variables used and the population to be studied would be included in this section.

Often in journal articles the introduction ends at this point. However, in some journal articles and most dissertations, the statement of the purpose is followed by a statement of the expected results of the study. These may be stated in terms of a formal research hypothesis or in terms of the questions that guided the research. (For a further discussion of hypotheses see Chapter 2.)

Two additional comments seem particularly important when writing introductions. First, considered as a whole, the introduction is organized in a V- or funnel-shaped fashion — that is, the introduction begins by dealing with a general consideration of important aspects of a research problem and proceeds to become more detailed and specific until the section ends with the questions to be answered by the research reported. Every empirical dissertation or article in psychology or education could begin with a history of psychology or education in America. That kind of focus would obviously be too broad. However, one is obliged to show that the problem and research the writer has done is relevant to the practice of psychology or education. So, the statement of the problem cannot be limited to, for example, a discussion of the methodological weaknesses of a body of research. This is one area in which the creativity and artistic skill of the writer is manifested in an introduction.

The second point to bear in mind while writing an introductory section is that it is not a review of the literature in dissertations. (An introduction may incorporate elements of a review of literature in a journal article.) Entire chapters are reserved for this purpose in these works, so the review of the literature and the introduction should not cover the same ground. This does not mean that references cannot be used in an introduction. However, the few references used should be either references that provide a historical or practical framework for the statement of the problem or references that deal with the one or two articles on which the present research is primarily based. The former are seldom referenced again in the literature review, while the latter are always reviewed, but in greater detail.

Typing the Introduction

Unlike all other sections or chapters of research reports the introduction is not titled. The section simply begins after the title. Also, the statement of the problem and the statement of the purpose need not be given subheadings. If the section includes the formal research hypothesis, then a subheading is desirable. The subheading is listed in the table of contents so that a reader can quickly locate the hypothesis.

REVIEW OF THE LITERATURE

The review of literature in a dissertation is the place where the student demonstrates a thorough knowledge of the most important research, opinion, and theory relating to his/her topic. It is not a compilation of every article relating to a topic. This would be impractical, since in some way much of the literature in psychology and education is inter-related. For example, if a student were interested in the relationship between self-esteem and achievement, to be exhaustive s/he would need to review the literature in social reinforcement, identification, level of aspiration, locus of control, etc., since all these relate in some way to self-esteem or to achievement. The review might not even be exhaustive in terms of the literature that specifically relates self-esteem to achievement. If 300 articles exist on this topic, many will not have added anything new to an understanding of the relationship because they utilized unsound methodologies or obsolete measures or reported much the same results as many of the other articles. Thus, a literature review is always selective, and it is in this selection that the artistic skill of the writer-researcher is seen.

Some students seek topics on which there has been little research, with the belief that the literature review will be shorter and thus more easily compiled and written. This is a mistaken notion, since the researcher must review related research even if it is not closely related to his/her topic. For example, if a researcher found that there was little research on the relationship between diagnostic skill and the diagnostician's quantitative ability, s/he would have to review literature that led him/her to believe this relationship was important. Thus, s/he might report on studies that found correlations between quantitative ability and concept formation, inductive or deductive reasoning, success in graduate school or success on the job. There is always a literature to review because the researcher is compelled to show the relationship between what s/he is doing and what has been done. The length of the review, then, has much less to do with the amount of previous research, opinion, or theory on a topic than it does with the space limitations on the writer or with his/her motivation.

Because the review of the literature is often the most lengthy chapter in a dissertation, there is a real necessity to stick to a structure that will help organize and integrate material discussed. Five or six techniques can be used to organize a review: (1) organizing material in a V or funnel fashion, (2) reporting on some studies in more detail than others, (3) using headings, (4) employing summary tables, (5) connecting sentences, and (6) summarizing.

In general, the literature review should be organized so that the more general material is discussed first, and the material most closely related to the research reported in the dissertation is discussed last. For example, a study of the relationship between student characteristics (achievement, IQ, locus of control, and sex) and student ratings of teacher competence might begin with a section on the social psychology of person perception or the historical trend toward teacher accountability. The review would culminate in a discussion of research on student characteristics as determinants of the ratings of teachers, particularly of studies that investigated the same set of student characteristics that were investigated in the research reported in the dissertation.

Continuing the previous example, if there were a number of studies relating student characteristics to student ratings of teachers, a separate subsection could be devoted to a discussion of studies that found a relationship between each one of the student variables and ratings of teachers. Thus, the review would have four or five subsections, each with a heading. The headings might be as follows:

The Theory of Person Perception

Relationship between Student Achievement and Student Ratings of Teachers

Relationship between Student Sex and Student Ratings of Teachers

Relationship between Student Locus of Control and Student Ratings of Teachers

Most graduate students have little trouble with the first two techniques of organizing a review; they divide the review into subheadings and organize the sections so that the most general topics are discussed first. However, within subsections the organization and integration of the material break down. There are four ways in which this problem can be avoided. First, the subsections of the review should be organized in a funnel structure. Thus, the section reviewing studies on the relationship between student achievement and student ratings of teachers should be organized so that the articles of historical interest or the articles utilizing different types of samples or procedures than those utilized by the reviewer are presented first. The more recent articles utilizing samples and procedures similar to those used by the reviewer are then presented.

Second, each article does not deserve the same degree of treatment. The most obvious sign of a poorly and hastily done review is one in which all the articles are given the traditional half-page treatment and in which something is said about the subjects, procedure, outcome, and discussion of each piece of research. As a rough guideline, the reviewer might want to divide his/her reviewed material in each subsection into three parts: (1) material that will be described in detail because it is highly related to the present study or is important for some other reason, e.g. it reports results contrary to the rest of the material reviewed, (2) material that will be briefly discussed, and (3) material that will simply be listed as replicates of one of the other two types of material. If only this one structural principle is utilized, much of the boredom generated by reading reviews of literature could be avoided.

There are some instances, particularly with topics on which there has been a large outpouring of research, where a summary table can be helpful. Such a table might look like Table I.

Some dissertation committees might find this kind of presentation too informal for the final copy of the dissertation. Though this might be the case, the student might find such a table helpful as a preliminary step in organizing the material of a review. Furthermore, this technique should not be used unless there are at least ten or twelve studies with similar outcomes to be reported. Finally, the student should not make a table if all the information contained in the table is going to be discussed in the text. A table should be used if only its high points are discussed in the text.

A more subtle but important device for integrating large amounts of information is the appropriate use of transition phrases that lead the reader's attention from one paragraph to the next. Such

TABLE I

STUDIES FINDING ADULT PRAISE SUPERIOR TO ADULT REPROOF
IN FOSTERING BEHAVIOR CHANGE

Author(s)	Subjects	Task	Follow-Up
Jones & Smith (1942)	1st and 2nd grade white, both sexes	verbal learning task	no
Smith & Novak (1964)	high school seniors males	motor skill task	yes; differences remained significant
Goldberg & Sanchez (1976)	3- and 4-year-olds both sexes	social approach responses	yes; differences not significant
etc.	etc.	etc.	etc.

transitions are present in all writing but become particularly important in reviews where long dicussions of similar types of material occur. The transition is usually a part of the topic sentence of the new paragraph. Some examples of poor transition phrases are listed below:

Another study that found that reproof was better than praise . . .

Smith, Kline, and French (1975) also found that reproof was better than praise.

Rosenberg (1975) utilized second graders from parochial schools to study the effects of reproof and praise.

The first two examples imply that the material is all of equal importance and that the material discussed is just one more building block supporting a particular point. If this is the only reason that the article is cited, this kind of transition may be appropriate. But, unless the new material adds something special to the previously cited material, it should probably be reported as follows:

Other researchers have obtained similar results (Smith, Kline, & French, 1975; Taylor, 1964; Zajonc, 1964).

The third example is inappropriate because it begins the description of the new material without attempting to tie it to what has already been reviewed. This sentence could be acceptable if somewhere in the paragraph the writer makes the connection between this material and the previously reviewed material; in other words, the transition does not have to be made in the first sentence of each paragraph (this may create a boring pattern), although this is the primary place in which it is made. Some examples of better transition phrases include the following:

> Geller's methodological weaknesses were avoided by Locke (1975) in his recent study of the expectancy effect.
>
> Mondale's subjects were all inner-city black children, and the extent to which his findings can be generalized is not clear. However, Hammill (1974) utilized a similar teaching technique with naturalized Puerto Rican children and obtained the same results.

The clarity and value of these introductory sentences is difficult to judge without seeing the remainder of the paragraphs to which they refer. However, they do have the advantage that they make a strong connection between what has already been reviewed and the material that follows.

The final device that can be used to integrate a review is the summary. It is most successfully used to point out the highlights of a subsection that the writer feels has been lengthy and complex. Some students find it difficult to write brief summaries of complex material because they feel the summary is an oversimplification. All summaries are oversimplifications, however, and they all sacrifice detail for the purpose of clarity. Since clarity is the major objective of a summary, the writer should use it as a criterion against which to judge the appropriate length and comprehensiveness of a summary.

METHOD

The most important chapter of a dissertation from the scientific point of view is the method chapter. The purpose of the methodology chapter is to explain what the researcher did to obtain the data s/he collected. If carefully done, the description of the research procedures allows other researchers to evaluate the quality of the results obtained and to attempt replication. Since this is the purpose, the methodology chapter is judged against two criteria, clarity and comprehensiveness.

In experimental laboratory research there is a long history of attention to detail in describing methodology. Most graduate students in psychology and education have read experimental research in which the strain of albino rat, loudness of apparatus noises, and illumination in the experimental setting were dutifully reported. With many good journals available publishing research of this type, most graduate students writing in basic research areas will have little difficulty discussing their procedures with precision.

The models available to the field researcher in psychology and education are generally less adequate. It is not difficult to find, for example, an article that compares three types of therapeutic interventions for school phobia (desensitization, client-centered therapy, and family therapy) the procedure section of which reports only the number and length of the therapy sessions and the sex and training of the therapist. In addition, a general description of the orientation of each therapist may be given. This type of reporting can seldom be justified, even under the space limitations imposed on journal articles. It is never justified in dissertation writing. The minimal acceptable description of each of these treatments would include a delineation of all the processes utilized in each type of therapy. For the desensitization procedure it would include descriptions of (1) how the fears that served as the target behavior were determined, (2) how the fear hierarchy was determined and constructed, (3) the actual desensitization procedure in detail (including number of trials per level of each hierarchy, number of hierarchies, techniques used to indicate anxiety level by the subject, length of exposure to each scene, etc.), and (4) the manner in which the *in vivo* test of the treatment was done. For the other therapeutic interactions where the processes may not be as easily identified, the researcher might include typed scripts from tapes of the sessions (or at least a time-sampled script) so that the processes outlined by the researcher can be verified. The point of this example is simply to reaffirm the necessity for comprehensive and precise reporting of the experimental methodology. Without it, any piece of empirical research is greatly weakened, regardless of the outcome of the investigation.

Although the methodology chapter of a dissertation is of central importance, it is perhaps the easiest to write from a structural point of view. The reason for this is that there is a long historical precedent for the format or structure of this chapter, and it is readily recognized by most graduate students in psychology and education. The following headings provide an outline of the typical method chapter:

Subjects
Design
Materials
Procedure

In some cases the Design section is omitted, but the remaining sections are almost always present.

Subjects

Within the subject section, the major decision revolves around how extensive the subject description should be. The answer to this question varies from project to project. However, the exact number of subjects tested or treated is always indicated, since this number has such a strong effect on the internal and external validity of the results of the investigation. Furthermore, since sex, age, and socioeconomic status have been found to be potent variables in psychological and educational research on children and adolescents, these variables are almost always described. Sex and age are fairly easily determined, but socioeconomic status may not be. This variable can be handled in one of three ways:

1. If the variables studied are not known to be highly related to socioeconomic status, then the researcher may simply subjectively describe the sample based on a general geographical area. For example, the sample consisted of sixty-four seven- and eight-year-old black children (thirty-two males, thirty-two females) from the inner-city section of a large eastern city. The area from which the children were selected has been designated by the federal government as a model cities area.

2. A slightly more refined technique for determining socioeconomic status is to utilize a governmental designation of the family of the subject or the peers of the subject. As an example of this, the sample consisted of sixty-four seven- and eight-year-old black children (thirty-two males, thirty-two females) who attended an elementary school that receives

Title I funds. Eighty-three percent of the children's families were receiving welfare compensation of one type or another, the predominate type being aid to dependent children.

3. The most rigorous technique for determining socioeconomic status is to calculate a socio-economic index using one of the systems in general use. Although it was developed in 1949 and is to some extent out of date, the Warner system is still the predominant system in use.[3] It utilizes occupation of mother and father, source of income (salary or inheritance), house type (apartment, private home), dwelling area (areas rated in terms of status), parental education, and income. The complete scale is difficult to use and thus is rarely used; two or three of the indices are probably satisfactory for most purposes. Even one index, if the data are reliable, is better than either of the alternate systems listed previously.

Other characteristics of children that often deserve careful delineation are IQ, grade level, and diagnostic classification (educable retarded, emotionally disturbed). In the case of IQ and diagnostic classification the assessment procedures used must be specified. Children, of course, can be classified or described in an almost infinite variety of ways so the research purpose alone determines which subject characteristics are most important.

The description of adults in psychological and

---

[3]Warner, W.L. *Social class in America.* New York: Harper & Row, 1960.

educational research is slightly different from that of children. Sex, age, and socioeconomic status remain important variables. However, if the researcher is describing a teacher or therapist sample, for example, socioeconomic status can be eliminated because occupation is one acceptable index of socioeconomic status (SES). Furthermore, age may not be as relevant as the years of experience of the subject in the profession. In describing teachers it is frequently helpful to report the grade level and general SES level of the teacher's students; also, the subject area being taught and the level of education of the teacher should be noted.

Design

In describing the design of a study the following information should be reported:

1. Describe the design of the study.
2. Name the variables studied and classify them as dependent and independent if this delineation is meaningful. State whether the variables are treated as nominal, ordinal, or interval data.
3. State whether subjects were randomly selected or randomly assigned to treatment.
4. Name the types of control groups that are used, if any.

Campbell and Stanley's classification of experimental and quasi-experimental designs can be very helpful in developing this description, since the classification takes into account most of the previously mentioned information. There is no need, however, for the student to go into a long description of the internal and external validity considerations of the design in the Design section of the paper. They should be understood and discussed with the committee but need not be discussed in writing in this section. They, may of course, be a major focus of the Discussion section.

A description of a design should not be confused with a description of a statistical analysis procedure. An analysis procedure may imply a design, but it is not a design. For example, a double classification analysis of variance or multiple regression are not designs; they are analysis procedures.

Materials

The materials section usually includes a description of the experimental setting, apparatus, and measurement devices. The characteristics of the experimental or measurement setting that require description are those that the researcher feels are relevant to the procedures carried out in that setting. In a task requiring quick responses to fast-moving visual stimuli, e.g. a pursuit task, such variables as subject distance from visual stimuli, room illumination, and presence of distracting noises may be important. If the task requires four children to sit around a table and work on a paper-and-pencil task, then the seating distance from subject to subject might be important, as well as the type and quantity of visual and auditory distractions. Like many other aspects of research reporting, no formula can be given to determine which characteristics of the setting to report. The researcher should be aware, however, that in most research some kind of setting characteristics should be reported.

The same generalization holds true in the cases where specially prepared measurement or task-presenting apparatuses are used. If, for example, a researcher was investigating the reliability and validity of a group-administered Bender Gestalt Test, and the forms to be copied by the subjects were presented by means of slide projections, then the type of projector, type of slide (color or black-and-white, line drawing or photograph), and size of slide image on the screen might be reported. These characteristics would be selected because they seem to have some relationship to the ability of the subject to see and copy the form presented.

Most research in psychology and education requires paper-and-pencil measurement devices of some sort. It is in the description of such devices that graduate students seem to have the most problems in the Materials section. The following is a list of characteristics that should be reported for most paper-and-pencil instruments:

1. Name of the instrument.
2. Name of author(s).
3. Purpose of the instrument (What is it a measure of?)
4. Number and name of the subscales of the instrument.
5. Number of items, and number of items for each subscale.
6. Response format (multiple choice, yes or no, Likert, open-ended, etc.).
7. Scoring of instrument (particularly important if some items are scored in a direction opposite to others).
8. Reliability (including some measure of internal consistency, test and retest, alternate forms, and interrater or interscorer reliability if applicable).

9. Validity (a review of the most important research relating the instrument to other constructs. Do not make this review into a lengthy discussion. If that much information is available and needed, incorporate a review of the validity of the instrument in the review of literature).

There are, of course, instruments to which the above list does not apply. The Wechsler Scales and the Stanford-Binet are so well known that some characteristics of the test (number of items and subscales, for example) may not need to be discussed. The validity issue for such instruments should not be totally dismissed, however; a review of some summary articles and expert opinion should be included. Of course, this abbreviated approach cannot be used when the subjects are members of a minority group.

The list does not apply to measurement devices such as observation instruments used in behavior modification style research. In this case, reliability is limited to a discussion of interrater reliability, and validity is not discussed. The validity of such instruments lies in the fact that a behavior being observed is precisely defined.

The description of the instrument should be augmented by a discussion of the person who administered the instrument. At minimum, the sex, race, age, and training of the test administrator should be described, since these variables have been shown to affect some types of paper-and-pencil responses.

If the student researcher prepares an original instrument to be used as a measurement device for the dissertation, s/he should carry out a pilot study and report the results of this study. The report should include number and characteristics of subjects used and the criterion used to select the original item pool and final pool. The latter criteria will include consideration of item difficulty, item-total correlations, and reliability considerations.

Procedure

The Procedure section of the Method chapter describes all pertinent aspects of the research process that have not been described in the Subjects, Design, and Materials sections. Specifically, it is devoted to a description of how and when the subjects and materials were utilized by the researcher. Since the temporal order of research events is an important aspect of the Procedure section, it is usually organized as a chronological description.

Although the specific points to be covered in the Procedure section vary somewhat depending on the type of research reported, the following is an example of some of the questions typically answered in this section:

1. How were the subjects brought together in the experimental setting, or how did the researcher obtain access to the subjects in the natural setting?
2. What were the subjects told about why they were chosen and about the purpose of the research?
3. If the research involved a treatment, in what ways were the experimental and control groups treated differently?
4. What instructions were the subjects given regarding the tasks or measures they were to complete?

5. In what order were the tasks or measures administered?
6. How many experimental sessions took place, what was their temporal spacing, and how long did each one last?
7. Were the subjects debriefed after the experimental session(s) as to the purpose of the research or the findings?

One of the decisions a researcher has to deal with when reporting procedure is the extent to which s/he provides verbatim transcriptions of the instructions to the subjects. In general, verbatim transcriptions should be included if the wording (as opposed to the general concepts) of the instructions is considered important. In research on social reinforcement, for example, it is not sufficient to say that the subjects were praised for improved performance—the researcher must report what words were used. A researcher doing classroom observation who asks the teacher to ignore him/her while s/he is observing need not report the exact words used in these instructions. Also, instructions for well-known measurement instruments need not be reported.

RESULTS

The Results chapter of a dissertation has as its purpose the presentation of the data obtained from the research instruments. Like all scientific writing, this chapter is judged against the criteria of comprehensiveness and clarity. However, this chapter is by definition a summary. It describes the results in terms of descriptive statistics (mean, median, mode, standard deviation, etc.) that summarize individual data points, not the individual data points themselves. Thus, clarity is the dominant characteristic of a well-written Results chapter.

Clarity, of course, requires a well-organized structural plan. Because of the emphasis given to training of psychologists and educators in methods of statistical analysis, there is a strong tendency to organize the chapter around the particular significance test used. In almost all cases, this is a poor choice. Because the hypotheses have already set a structure; the reader wants to know the answer to each of the questions raised by the researcher. Also, results of a research effort are the raw data and the descriptive statistics associated with that data. The result is not the outcome of the decision rule incorporated in the inferential statistic (the test of significance). If the reader has doubts about the latter point, s/he should remember that programs of research often must rely on nonsignificant trends to indicate possibly productive future research areas. This is necessary because of the low strength of most psychological variables related to the amount of uncontrolled variance and the close association between sample size and statistical significance.

For these reasons a more satisfactory structure for the presentation of results can be built around hypotheses than around the statistical analysis. The following is an outline of such a structure:

1. State of the first hypothesis: The first hypothesis of this study states that there is a positive relationship between IQ and academic achievement measured by numerical grades given by teachers in grades one through nine.
2. Reference the table or figure that contains the summary statistics relevant to this hypothesis:

Table I presents the correlation between IQ and achievement for each grade level.

3. Describe the highlights of the data contained in this table: It can be seen that all the correlations contained in Table I are in a positive direction and range from .09 to .89. The average correlation is .61.

4. State what test was used to test the significance of the data: Each correlation in this table was tested for significance by means of the Fisher r to z transformation (McNemar, 1966, p. 137).

5. State the outcome of the analysis: In all cases but one (the correlation between IQ and achievement for grade one) the correlation was significant at the .05 level.

6. State whether or not the hypothesis was supported or not by the direction of the data and the statistical test: Since all the correlations were in a positive direction and all but one were significantly different from zero, the first hypothesis is given substantial support.

7. State next hypothesis: The second hypothesis states that the correlation between IQ and achievement will decrease from the first grade to the tenth grade level.

8. Etc.

A number of additional pieces of information may be included in the Results section. These include descriptions of assumptions of statistical tests, descriptions of the kinds of data that will be used (e.g. in a pretest-posttest design are posttest scores, change scores, or posttest scores with pretest scores serving as the covariante used), description of *post hoc* tests, and subsidiary analyses.

Many dissertations and theses contain a section devoted to the delineation of the assumptions of the statistical tests used and the procedures used to test the assumptions of the statistics. The placement of this discussion depends on how many different statistical procedures are used. If there is only one major statistical procedure, the assumptions and the tests of the assumptions should be presented before the first hypothesis is discussed. With this out of the way, the reader can get to the major questions without stumbling over two pages of statistical discussion. If, on the other hand, a different procedure is used for two or more hypotheses, then after the appropriate statistics are introduced (step 4 above), the discussion of the assumptions takes place. The student should not dwell at great length on the assumptions and their tests. Some brevity here is justified so that the important business of presenting the results of the experiment can be attended to. However, the student should be aware of the details of the assumptions and their tests so that s/he can defend his/her statistical procedures. (This will greatly reduce anxiety during the oral defense.)

Other kinds of discussions may also find their place in the beginning of the Results section, or they may be slotted into the discussion of each hypothesis, depending on their generality. For example, one often has to discuss the manner in which missing data, ceiling effects on measures, or subject absence are dealt with in the data analysis, or one might have to indicate what type of data were utilized in the analysis (posttest scores, regressed posttest scores, etc.). If they seem to apply to all or most of the hypotheses, they should be discussed at the beginning of the chapter. If not, they should be discussed in the appropriate subsection under each hypothesis.

In many dissertations, relationships between variables that are not covered by the hypotheses are of interest. For example, in a study of the effects on achievement of three independent variables (e.g. self-concept, neuroticism, and locus of control), there may be interest in assessing the relationships among the three independent variables, even though these relationships are not the subjects of hypotheses. The author would feel free to report these relationships after the main hypotheses have been addressed. A section of the Results chapter in which nonhypothesized relationships are discussed is sometimes called the Subsidiary Analysis section.

Another example of the use of this section is when a researcher finds s/he wants to modify his/her measures because s/he did not get results supporting the hypotheses. S/he might want to remove subjects who seemed to understand the purpose of the study, to remove data taken from questionnaires that were only partially completed, or to eliminate items of low reliability from a pencil-and-paper measure and test the hypotheses on the rescored measure. S/he should not include such analyses in the main Hypothesis Testing section of the Results chapter but should feel free to try out ideas in the Subsidiary Analysis section.

It was stated earlier that a Results section is judged primarily in terms of clarity. One way to achieve clarity is to eliminate material from this section that is not absolutely necessary for the understanding of the outcome of the research. One technique that may be helpful in this regard is to put all tables and figures that do not seem necessary in the Index of the paper. In this way they are present if an interested reader wants further details on a particular matter, but they do not clutter the Results section to a point that the reader cannot follow the text. Material often treated this way includes formula derivations for rarely used statistics, listings of individual data or raw scores, and detailed breakdowns of data that are already handled in summary form. Source tables for *F* and *t* tests can be handled in the same way.

Clarity is also achieved by eliminating redundant information. In particular, the student should not create a table if every piece of data in the table is going to be discussed. A table is a presentation device, and the text should be used to summarize it. Also, the student should use figures (photographs, line drawings, graphs) sparingly. They are expensive to make and reproduce and are often redundant. The exception to this rule is in research involving small samples, such as research in behavior modification, in which case figures constitute the data analysis tool.

Finally, the student should not interpret results in the Results section except to say whether they support or do not support the hypotheses. Specifically, s/he should not say that a particular result supports or does not support the findings of another researcher. This type of discussion will be handled in the Discussion chapter.

DISCUSSION

The Discussion section of a dissertation is that section in which the researcher indicates the meaning and import of the findings s/he has reported in the Results section. Like the Introduction, it is a difficult chapter to write because it calls for discussion of material that is more remotely related to the present research than the material presented in the Methods and Results chapters. It is not simply a summarization of the words of others as in the Review chapter. The Discussion chapter calls for a good deal of self-generated material, which taxes the creativity of the best researcher.

The overall structure of the discussion is the familiar V-shaped pattern, but unlike the Introductory and Review chapters, which begin with general concerns and proceed to the more specific, the Discussion section is organized in the opposite fashion — that is, the topics covered proceed from the specific to the general.

Specifically, the Discussion chapter is organized into five units: (1) summary of results, (2) discussion of reasons for negative results, if they are obtained, (3) theoretical implications of results, (4) practical implications of results, and (5) suggestions for further research.

The summary of results can be handled in two ways, either by summarizing all the results or by summarizing the results on a hypothesis-by-hypothesis basis. This choice is governed by the complexity of the results. A study addressing six hypotheses may be difficult to summarize in global terms. The selection of the global or hypothesis-by-hypothesis procedure is important in that other units of the discussion may have to follow the organizational pattern set by the results summary. For example, if a researcher had several hypotheses, some of which were supported and some of which were not, s/he might wish to discuss the reasons for the negative findings, the theoretical and practical implications of the findings, and even the suggestions for further research under each hypothesis. Such a process would be somewhat cumbersome, however. What is frequently done is to summarize the results, discuss the reasons for the negative results, and point out the theoretical implications of the results on a hypothesis-by-hypothesis basis. Then, s/he can treat in a global manner the practical implications of the results and suggestions for further research. Almost any organization of these units is permissible if the reader can easily follow the line of reasoning.

When results are obtained that were not expected or were not hypothesized, the researcher is required to attempt to explain the outcome. This obligation stems from the fact that the Introduction and Literature Review have explained why a certain outcome should occur. The explanation of negative findings is by nature speculative and tentative. It usually takes the form of a criticism of the research procedure. For example, persons engaging in survey research typically explain negative results by pointing out the lack of a 100 percent return rate. Since most researchers obtain a 20 to 40 percent return rate, the results could always have resulted from a systematic selection factor regarding those who returned the questionnaire versus those who did not. In experimental research the potency of the treatment or the length of time it was applied is frequently questioned. Other types of "typical explanations" of negative results involve ceiling effects on some measure, subject knowledge of the experimental hypotheses, failure of an experi-

menter to follow experimental directions, or inter-
vening natural occurrences that interrupt data collection or the experimental treatments (school
strikes, competing school programs, subject illness,
etc.). In general, such explanations point to some
internal validity problem of the research design.

The theoretical implication of a research finding
is the area most often slighted in dissertation research. It involves a discussion of how the obtained
finding coincides with other researcher's findings
and how well the finding coincides with the theory
or theories guiding the research. For example, if
one found that black children performed more
poorly on a test of visual perception than white
children, results could be explained using a structural insult theory (black children have poorer
health services, thus they have more brain damage)
or by a learning discrimination theory (black children have not been taught to respond differentially
to abstract symbols to the same extent as white
children). In this case, since both explanations are
possible, they should both be discussed. Sometimes
a study is devised to help the researcher decide
between the appropriateness of two theories. In this
case the discussion of theoretical implications is
easier, since it has been the focus of the research
from the start. The theoretical implications discussion then becomes the major focus of the Discussion
chapter.

Another area where graduate students often find
trouble is in the specification and exploration of
practical implications of a research finding. However, unlike the undertreatment often given theoretical implications, the tendency is generally to
find more practical implications than are justified.

A favorite question of oral examiners is "What do you think your data mean for the day-to-day practice of psychology and education?" Nearly always the answer should be "very little." The temptation to overemphasize practical implications can be avoided by appropriate qualification of statements about these implications and by pointing out what kinds of research should be done to build this finding into one with real practical import.

This brings us to the final section of the discussion, the suggestions for future research. Such suggestions stem from two types of limitations of almost all research — limitations in terms of internal and external validity. Internal validity limitations revolve around limitations of the methodology. External validity limitations revolve around questions of whether the results can be generalized to subjects other than the subjects in the sample studied. Since no research deals with the entire population of interest and tests the treatment(s) under all necessary conditions, it is a compromise and must deal with limitations of researcher time and money. Thus, there are always internal validity and external validity limitations. The properly prepared section on suggested future research, however, does not simply catalogue all the research that seems necessary to answer a question; it suggests only that research that in the mind of the writer has the greatest possibility of being fruitful. Typical suggestions include carrying out the same procedure on different populations, refining the treatment in some way, or studying the effect of the dependent variable in conjunction with some other dependent variables thought to interact with the first variable in a significant way.

SUMMARY

1. The Introduction section includes the statements of the problem and purpose of the research and, typically, the hypotheses. The problem subsection describes the practical and theoretical importance of the research carried out, and the purpose subsection briefly discusses the guiding principles that determined the nature of the research done.

2. The Introduction is organized in a V format—that is, the discussion proceeds from the general to the specific, terminating with a brief description of the specific questions that were addressed by this research effort.

3. The Review of the Literature is a discussion of the most relevant research in an area. It is often divided into topic areas, and every topic area is structured according to the V format discussed in point 2 above.

4. Because reviews are lengthy and complex and are, therefore, difficult to read and understand, the writer must use devices such as summary tables, periodic summary discussions, and well-designed connecting sentences to reduce reader confusion.

5. More than any other section of a dissertation, the Method section is judged against the criteria of clarity, precision, and comprehensiveness.

6. The Method section includes a discussion of subjects, design, materials, setting, and procedure.

7. In most cases the discussion of the results of research efforts should be organized accord-

ing to the hypotheses or questions to be answered, not according to data analysis procedures.

8. Discussion sections are organized around five topics, including (1) a summary of results, (2) a discussion of reason for negative results, (3) theoretical implications of results, (4) practical implications of results, and (5) suggestions for further research.

Chapter 4

SELF-CONTROL TECHNIQUES AND THE DISSERTATION

The Problem

A student, whom we will call Bob, had completed all his class requirements for a doctoral degree very quickly. He had performed exceptionally well in all didactic, clinical, and practical experiences in his educational psychology training program. During the last semester of full-time course work he had had several discussions with a prospective dissertation chairman about a topic and had received a good deal of support for his ideas. After taking his doctoral qualifying examinations, he obtained a full-time job with a suburban school district as head of the special services department, which occupied a good deal of his time. His wife soon became pregnant, and preparations for the arrival of his first child and coping emotionally with the new family addition required more of his time.

At the end of his first year, after all course work had been completed, he had not submitted one draft of a dissertation proposal. He apologetically called his advisor, discussing all his time commitments and promising a proposal during the next semester. After several months had passed, he made an appointment with the advisor, talked about the projected research, and promised a proposal within a month or two. Six months later no proposal had been submitted.

Although this case is fictional, the scenario is well known to all dissertation advisors. It is so common that academic departments and university graduate schools typically institute policies regarding the length of time a person may be registered for dissertation credit *before being terminated.* Such policies produce enough fear to motivate some students to complete their projects but fail to motivate a significant number of others to appropriate behavior. One reason that such policies fail is that they have a history of being poorly enforced, since the consequences are so devastating for the individual and embarrassing for the institution.

Why is it that advanced graduate students fail to complete a dissertation project when they have performed well in other aspects of their educational careers? Some of the answers are touched on in the introduction to this manual.

Several additional factors contribute to this problem, also. The student at this stage of his/her professional development usually has marketable skills. Thus, given the costs of an education and current economic conditions, the student is pushed to find professional employment before the dissertation is complete. As in the preceding example, too, this is often a time of substantial marital responsibilities marriage, growing families, etc. For these reasons time for the dissertation is limited.

Also, the student has typically not had to cope with a task the size and complexity of a dissertation. S/he attempts to cope with it by infrequent bursts of activity on holidays or weekends. This is a very poor strategy for tasks as large as the dissertation.

Finally, the student working on a dissertation must be able to tolerate an extremely long delay of reinforcement. There are few rewards for work prior to the completion of the project. Also, like artists, novelists, and many other creative persons, there are few, if any, institutional supports for work production. There is no eight-to-five schedule, no daily supervision, no imposed work quota.

For a number of reasons, including the inordinate delay of reinforcement, Pear (in Wallace, 1977) has pointed out that novel writing is an "uncommon endeavor and, when it is undertaken, appears quite susceptible to extinction" (p. 515). The same can be said of writing about independent research, like that involved in dissertations.

SOME SOLUTIONS

What help or advice can then be given to the student whose work on his/her dissertation has bogged down, who is not producing a dissertation despite a fervent desire to do so? Five rather simple ideas will be provided; the ideas are based on the principles of self-applied or self-managed behavior modification (Pear; in Wallace, 1977). However, these principles have been practiced by craftsmen, artists, and the best students for as long as there have been craftsmen, artists, and good students.

Point I

The student must schedule regular and frequent work periods.

The student must sit down and realistically assess time commitments. S/he then can set aside several blocks of time to work on the dissertation project each week. The blocks of time need not be large. The amount of the time allotted depends on time availability and ability of the student to sit and work at one type of task. The author finds that blocks of two hours are most convenient for him. They allow enough time to concentrate on the task but do not produce lasting fatigue or the feeling that the task is aversive.

Even if a person's time schedule allows for only two or three such blocks of time per week, in a few weeks, major demonstrable progress can be made. Wallace (1977) quotes Anthony Trollope, a nineteenth century writer of over fifty novels, who says the following: "It has the force of the water-drop that hollows the stone. A small daily task, if it be really daily, will beat the labors of a spasmodic Hercules" (p. 518).

Paul Horgan (1973) in *Approaches to Writing* also talks about the importance of a "habit of work" that the apprentice writer must learn.

. . . not only will they study the technical details of their craft in this period of apprenticeship — they will learn also the habit of work without which the writer will never be more than an amateur. It is this habit of work which will bring the writer to his work table every day at the same hour, there to do about the same amount of work according to the capacity which experience tells him is naturally his. It is this habit of work which will teach him to learn the hazardous and challenging necessity of keeping alive . . . a work . . . which may take many months or even years to complete. (pp. 4–5)

Point II

The work of planning a research effort, of writing the proposal or dissertation, should take place in the same place each day, and this place should have characteristics conducive to this kind of work.

Behavior analysis has documented the fact that if a behavior is carried out repeatedly in one setting, the setting will come to be associated with that behavior and will tend to foster the continued occurrence of that behavior. Thus, when we lie down on a bed or couch, we tend to relax and fall asleep because this setting is associated with sleep on a daily basis. The establishment of this kind of stimulus control over behavior is the basis for the recommendation to work at one spot every day. It is best if this spot is reserved exclusively for this kind of work and similar academic work.

A major problem occurs when a setting is used for two incompatible behaviors. In such cases stimulus control works against such behaviors instead of supporting them. The student who attempts to study in bed may well find that s/he tends to fall asleep while studying or find his/her mind actively pursuing some academic thought while attempting to sleep. Thus kitchen tables and soft comfortable chairs used for relaxing are poor places to work.

The setting, of course, should also have characteristics that are conducive to concentrated effort. It should be as free of auditory and visual distractions (family noises, radio, TV) as possible. Trying to work in front of a large window or in the traffic pattern of the home is not ideal.

Again, professional writers seem to understand the relationship between the work setting and work output. Ernest Hemmingway, for example, reportedly worked in one part of his home, standing at the typewriter everyday. He stood because he found that if he sat he relaxed and his attention wandered.

Point III

A goal should be set for the amount of work to be produced each day or each week and a record should be kept of the amount of work accomplished in order to determine if the goal has been met.

Keeping records of the amount of time one spends in a particular activity serves two functions. First, it makes one aware of exactly how much time is spent working on the task. Such awareness helps to eliminate the self-delusion that one is accomplishing more than, in reality, s/he is. People frequently say they have worked all day at a particular task when in fact they worked for an hour, took a two-hour break, worked for another hour, took a lunch break, etc. Like the overweight person who nibbles between meals then states that s/he does not understand why s/he cannot lose weight because s/he eats such small meals, the student will tend to make overly optimistic assessments of how much time s/he has spent at the writing desk, and this will tend to hinder understanding why little progress is being made on the project.

In addition to improving self-awareness, record keeping serves as a motivational device. If one has set a realistic goal for daily page production and has not met that goal, this fact prods and pushes the record keeper to improve his/her performance. Also, a small improvement in the amount of work accomplished during a given week will be a strong reinforcer; such improvement might have gone unnoticed if careful records were not kept.

Irving Wallace (1977), a contemporary novelist,

reports that he keeps detailed records of how much he has written.

With my fifth book, I started keeping a more detailed chart, which also showed how many pages I had written by the end of every working day. I am not sure why I started keeping such records. I suspect that it was because as a free-lance writer, entirely on my own, without employer or deadline, I wanted to create disciplines for myself, ones that were guilt making when ignored. A chart on the wall served as such a discipline; its figures scolding me or encouraging me. (p. 516)

Ernest Hemingway (Plimpton, in Wallace, 1977) also kept records of work production. He keeps track of his daily progress — "so as not to kid myself" — on a large chart made out of the side of a cardboard packing case and set up against the wall under the nose of a gazelle head. The numbers on the chart showing the daily output of words differ from 450, 575, 462, 1250, back to 512, the higher figures on days Hemingway put in extra work so he won't feel guilty spending the following day fishing on the Gulf Stream. (p. 519)

Point IV

Supplement reinforcement if necessary.

Although daily or weekly record keeping provides frequent reinforcement for completion of small units of work in the form of satisfaction for work accomplished, sometimes extra incentives or punishments are necessary. As in the Hemingway example quoted before, such reinforcements may consist of allowing oneself to spend time doing a pleasurable activity if the goal for the week has been met. Other rewards, such as buying oneself a small luxury, or contracting with others to perform one of the undesirable household chores, may prove to be the best motivational devices.

Harris (1974) reports on a program to help a thirty-three-year-old assistant professor complete her dissertation which utilized a technique referred to as a deposit contract. The procedures used were based on the work of Nurnberger and Zimmerman (1970), who also worked with a student attempting to complete a dissertation. The subject, in the Harris example, had completed all work for a Ph.D. in mathematics except the dissertation and had secured a position with a university. She had completed all work for her dissertation one year after taking the university position but for two years had not been able to write it.

The program worked out for the subject involved giving fifty dollars in five-dollar bills to a friend. Each bill was placed in a stamped envelope addressed to a prosely tizing church organization that the subject intensely disliked. A contract was drawn up between the subject and her friend specifying that if five or more pages were not submitted each week, the envelope would be put in the mail to the church. If five or more pages did appear, the envelope would be returned to the subject.

The subject produced ten pages the first week, four the second, and none the third because of illness. The third week was excused, but the envelope was mailed to the church the second week. The fourth and fifth weeks no work appeared either, so the envelopes were mailed. On the sixth week, six new pages were presented, but on the seventh nothing was produced. On the eighth week the subject appeared with a forty eight-page draft of the entire dissertation in hand. The contingencies were stopped pending the response of her committee to the draft. Six weeks after her committee had returned her first draft with corrections to be made, she had still not made the corrections. A new contract was therefore drawn up betwen the subject and her friend that specified that the three remaining envelopes with five dollars in each would be sent six, eleven, and thirteen days late if the revisions had not been made. Also, a note was to be enclosed in the envelopes asking for one of the church members to call upon the subject. Six days later all revisions were made. The dissertation was soon accepted and the subject received her Ph.D. the following summer.

Although this example may seem extreme, such measures have been used by professional writers to enhance their own motivation. Perhaps the most colorful example is that of Victor Hugo, who is reported to have confined himself to his study for a given period every day by ordering his servant to take away all his clothing and not to return it until the time he was to finish writing that day (Wallace, 1977, p. 518).

Point V

Anticipate lower rates of production after a large segment of work has been completed.

Working on a project like a dissertation has much in common with an experimental situation studied by psychologists in which an animal or a human subject must make a large number of responses before receiving a reinforcement (referred

to as ratio reinforcement, because of the relationship or ratio between the fixed number of responses
made and the number of reinforcement administered), the organism tends to stop responding for a
while after a reinforcement has been given. It is as
if the organism realizes that efforts immediately
after a reinforcement will not be rewarded, so it is
difficult to get started on the large amount of work
needed to receive the next reward. If tests are given
in a college class every eight weeks, for example,
this pattern is often observed, for students tend to
study very little immediately after a test, but their
rate of study increases as the next test approaches.

An analysis of the writing charts of Irving Wallace reveals that for each of his three novels for
which daily data were available (*The Prize, The
Man, The Plot*), the rate of writing per day tended
to follow the fixed-ratio pattern. That is, he wrote
at a relatively low rate at the beginning of each
novel and at an increasingly higher rate toward the
end (Wallace, 1977).

The author's informal observations of students
working on dissertations is that the work for the
project can be divided into three parts: from no
idea to formal acceptance of a proposal, from
acceptance of the proposal through data collections, and from data collections to the final write
up of the project. It is the author's feeling that the
amount of time spent on the project per week is
small at the beginning of each of these phases and
becomes progressively larger as the end of the
phases near completion. Furthermore, he feels that
most students have a harder time at the beginning
of the proposal stage producing a reasonable work
rate than they do at the beginning of the third

phase — writing the dissertation. This speculation is subject to empirical investigation and should be researched.

Knowing that this scalloping effect of effort over time is likely to occur, the student can take steps to minimize it. One step might be to institute a fairly strong reinforcement program for effort during these expected low periods of production. Special self-rewards of privileges or other reinforcers are particularly needed during these periods and are not needed at the end of each phase because the anticipation of completion is such a powerful reward. Even if external self-rewards are not used, the student should be aware of when low production rates are likely to occur, if only to minimize frustration and self-doubt.

AN APPROACH TO WRITING

Although a method of approaching a large writing task has been implicit at other points in this manual, it seems important to make this approach more explicit. The proposal and the dissertation usually cannot be written in one or two drafts. To attempt to do this is to attempt such a difficult task that most people fail to accomplish it. As Trumble (1975) has said, "The grim reality (is) that nine-tenths of all writing is rewriting" (p. 21). The student should think in terms of four or more drafts, each one concentrating on a different aspect of writing.

Appropriate preparation to write eliminates many writing problems. Such preparation primarily involves stockpiling a large amount of material about which to write. All writers need facts, references, examples, and quotations, and the writer of a research proposal or dissertation needs more of this material than almost any other writer. Particularly what is needed is solid, highly relevant material that bears directly on the ideas to be discussed. Confidence in writing comes, in part, from confidence in the knowledge that one has plenty of good ideas to write about. "Moral: If you have just enough solid data to work with, you don't have enough. If you have a big surplus of data, you are primed to write" (Trimble, 1975, p. 7).

Once the appropriate data are prepared, the first draft is an exercise in jotting down on paper those ideas that seem most relevant to the chapter or section to be written. Little attempt should be made to organize the material; ideas should be written down in the fashion of brainstorming. Outline form is useful to some people as a way to do this initial draft, but the ordering of material should not be overly emphasized.

The focus of the second draft is organization. Once the ideas have been laid out, an attempt must be made to order the material in a satisfying fashion. This ordering may be along a temporal-historical dimension, a conceptual dimension, or according to some other schema. Chapters 2 and 3 discussed many suggestions on how to order the sections of a proposal and a dissertation so the details will not be repeated here. Some professional writers prepare two or three different drafts, each one ordering their material in a different way so that they can choose from these the most satisfying organizational plan.

The third draft should focus on continuity between sentences and paragraphs. The appropriate ordering of material in previous drafts contributes greatly to continuity but is not sufficient. What is required is careful consideration of the initial sentences of each paragraph and how these sentences guide the reader from paragraph to paragraph. It also requires careful consideration of connecting words, e.g. since, however, because, still, therefore and phrases, e.g. on the other hand, within each paragraph that links one sentence to its predecessor.

The final draft is devoted to spelling, punctuation, and concern about grammar. This draft is sometimes left to an editor by professional writers who have access to such expertise. It is the least creative, most mechanical aspect of writing. The dissertation student should carry out a revision, checking for these aspects of writing but might also submit a draft to a person with expertise in this area for additional advice. Of course, good editors help with transitions, continuity, word choice, and other aspects of writing in addition to rules of grammar, punctuation, and spelling.

SUMMARY

1. Schedule regular and frequent work periods.
2. Work in the same place, if possible, each day. Make sure the work setting has characteristics conducive to concentrated effort, such as freedom from auditory and visual distraction.
3. A goal should be set for the amount of work to be produced each day or each week. A record must be kept of the amount of work accomplished, or amount of time spent at work, in order to determine if the goal has been met.
4. Utilize supplementary reinforcements for work completed, if necessary.

5. Anticipate lower rates of production after a large segment of work has been completed.
6. Count on writing four drafts (or more) of each section written. The first draft should focus on generation of ideas, the second on organization of ideas, the third on continuity between paragraphs and sentences, and the fourth on grammar, spelling, and punctuation.

References

Harris, M. B. Accelerating dissertation writing: case study. *Psychological Reports,* 1974, *34*, 984-986.

Horgan, P. *Approaches to writing.* New York: Farrar, Straus & Giroux, 1973.

Nurnberger, J. I., & Zimmerman, J. Applied analysis of human behavior: an alternative to conventional motivational inferences and unconscious determination in therapeutic programming. *Behavior Therapy,* 1970, *1*, 59-69.

Trimble, J. R. *Writing with style.* Englewood Cliffs, N. J.: Prentice-Hall, 1975.

Wallace, I. (with J. J. Pear). Self-control techniques of famous novelists. *Journal of Applied Behavior Analysis,* 1977, *10*, 515-525.

Chapter 5

THE ORAL DEFENSE

The oral defense has its origins in the European tradition in which the student "read" in an area of his/her discipline, then wrote a treatise about some aspect of that discipline. As opposed to the typical graduate student in the United States who attends classes in a highly structured program of study, who takes frequent examinations, and whose research is closely supervised by faculty, the traditional European student pursued a much less structured program of study, took examinations infrequently, and may have worked on his/her terminal research with little supervision from faculty. The oral defense in this tradition had an importance and a quality that is not typical in modern American universities. It was the major evaluation not only of the student's research but of his/her entire education.

The oral defense of a dissertation has some of the characteristics of its European ancestor, but it is altered by the fact that the student's progress has been closely monitored at all stages of his/her education including the period throughout his/her terminal research project. Since dissertation committees wish to avoid the embarrassment of having one of their students perform poorly on such a defense, they help the student prepare a product that they feel will be acceptable to the academic community in general.

If a dissertation committee has supervised and approved of a research project and the manner in which the project was written, what then is the purpose of the oral defense? There seem to be three. First, not all students seek out the opinions of their committee on a frequent basis, fearing perhaps the criticisms that may be made. Such students do themselves an injustice since the oral defense then takes on a more traditional form, for the student cannot be assured of the support of his/her committee. The other side of this problem is that some committees do not take their supervision responsibilities as seriously as the faculty at large would like. The oral defense takes place in the presence of faculty other than the student's committee, and these additional faculty members are officially sanctioned to serve as an examination committee; the examining committee, then, serves as a check on the dissertation committee's judgement that the student's work is acceptable.

A third purpose of an oral defense is to assess the student's ability to express himself/herself orally in an academic forum. A student may carry out an acceptable project but be unable to summarize the findings, implications, and shortcomings in a coherent fashion to a group of scholars. The oral defense provides practice and, usually, feedback on this important skill.

PERSONS PRESENT AT THE ORAL DEFENSE

In most universities the committee that helped the student prepare the master's thesis or doctoral dissertation and at least two additional faculty members must attend the oral defense. The members attending who are not part of the student's committee are referred to as the examining committee. This committee serves as the primary examining body during the oral examination. The rules for membership of this committee and methods of selection vary from one university to another; however, a typical procedure is to require that at least one of the examining committee members be from a department other than the student's major department. The examining committee is most often chosen by the chairperson of the student's committee with the student having the opportunity to veto the election of members with whom s/he feels uncomfortable.

One of the members of the examination committee is asked to chair the proceedings. The functions of the chairperson are to orient the student to the agenda of the oral defense and to control the floor of the meetings. Various procedures are used to select this chairperson, one of which is to allow the person from outside the student's department to chair the meeting. The rationale for this procedure is that it minimizes the possibility or appearance of bias toward the student.

In addition to the persons who must attend an oral defense, other faculty and often students are allowed to attend. Usually, any faculty within the university may attend an oral defense. It is considered to be a public event within the community of scholars. Graduate students are often encouraged to attend, also, in order to become familiar with the procedures of the defense or simply to profit from the candidate's expertise in a given content area. Since many students approach the oral defense with a good deal of anxiety, it is customary for other graduate students who wish to attend the defense to obtain the candidate's permission to do so. Many students have no misgivings about the attendance of other students, but some do, and this courtesy may help prevent the examined student from feeling overwhelmed by a´large number of persons attending the defense or may prevent the special pressure brought about by being examined under the scrutiny of one's personal friends and associates.

FORMAT OF THE ORAL DEFENSE

The defense of a dissertation can be divided into four phases: introduction of the candidate and the topic, description of the research project, questions from examiners, and decision making on the adequacy of the project and the defense.

The first step in any oral examination is taken when the chairperson of the examination committee asks the candidate to tell the group assembled about his/her professional background and how s/he became interested in the topic of his/her research. The purpose of the brief autobiographical sketch is simply to introduce the candidate to those assembled, many of whom may not have had previous contact with the candidate. The second part of the introduction serves the function of making the connection between the candidate's experience, intellectual interests, and future aspirations and the area of concern of his/her research.

No one has ever failed an oral examination because s/he has failed to introduce himself/herself or the topic well. However, should the student feel that s/he has gotten off to a less than graceful start, this may adversely affect the later presentation. The introduction should be kept very brief. The background information most useful to the examining group is that which is highly relevant to the professional preparation of the candidate, including educational and practical experience. As is the case in all other aspects of the defense, the candidate should cover only the highlights; if the examiners want to know more about some aspect of the student's preparation, they will ask. The student will find it helpful to practice his/her introduction once or twice before the day of the defense.

Summarizing the Project.

After the student has introduced himself/herself, the chairperson of the examining committee will usually ask the student to present a summary of his/her study. Although the candidate should plan to describe all major aspects of the study—the problem, purpose, hypotheses, method, results, and interpretation—the guiding principles of this description should be clarity and brevity. This task, if it has not been practiced by the student, will be difficult. The student has generally been working on the project for at least a year. S/he has struggled through a variety of theoretical and practical problems and can extemporaneously discuss many of these problems in detail. However, to be able to place each issue in context, to eliminate some issues completely, and to summarize the remaining issues in a few sentences requires great skill. This is a skill that many mature scientists and professionals have not mastered, as attendance at any professional meeting will demonstrate.

The bulk of the time of the oral defense should be spent on topics of interest to the examining committee and to the other persons present. The best tactic, then, is for the candidate to allow the audience to select those areas to discuss in detail by their questions. An example will perhaps illustrate the point. Most graduate students have qualms about the methodological aspect of their research. These stem from the fact that they have been trained primarily as content specialists (specialists in an area of an intellectual discipline or profession) not as methodological specialists. Because of their concerns about research design or statistics, they tend to focus most of their summary on these issues. If the examining committee, who has usually read the dissertation before the oral defense, feels that these aspects of the research were handled adequately, they may have little interest in such a discussion. Thus, because of anxiety the student is discussing material in which the committee has no interest and to which the audience has little desire to listen. How much better it is to list the statistical procedures utilized and move on to the major outcomes of the project. If someone is concerned about the manner in which each assumption of each statistical procedure was tested, then the candidate should be prepared to discuss these points. To burden those not interested with these details is wasteful with time that can be used on topics of importance.

Questions from Examiners

Dissertations vary in their strengths and weaknesses and, therefore, the focus of faculty questioning in a given research project varies considerably. The focus of these questions also is determined by the interests and areas of expertise of the examiners. However, experience indicates that students have a poor understanding of the types of questions that are most frequently asked in oral defenses.

The primary mistake made in psychology and

education is to prepare for methodological questions, particularly questions regarding statistical issues, to the neglect of other more fundamental issues. This focus of the student's preparation results, apparently, from a combination of the following elements: (1) general mathematical phobia, on the part of the student; (2) the fact that research training often emphasizes statistical issues; and (3) the security the student feels because the content or subject matter of the dissertation is more a direct outgrowth of his/her interests and professional training. In any event, the anxiety caused by statistical issues results in disproportionate preparation in this area.

Faculty members tend to place more emphasis in their questioning on the basic issues of the project. These issues include: (1) Why was this project worth doing? What did the student researcher expect to learn that was not already known, and why was this important knowledge to obtain? (2) What did the student learn from the research? (3) What implications do these findings have for the theoretical foundations of the concepts researched? (4) What are the practical implications of the research: (5) What weaknesses in research design limit the meaningfulness or the extent the research can be generalized? (6) What kinds of research need to be carried out to further clarify the questions that were asked by this researcher and the questions that were generated by his/her research?

In asking these questions the examining committee is simply attempting to determine if the student has isolated an important question, has systematically attempted to answer that question, and has understood to what extent the research carried out answers the question. These kinds of questions can readily be answered if the proposal for the research was clearly thought out and written and the introductory and concluding chapters of the dissertation were clearly thought out and written.

Perhaps the most difficult questions regarding any research are the extent to which the findings can be generalized and the delineation of practical implications that seem to be logical outgrowths of the research. If in doubt, the student in an oral defense should err on the side of conservatism; that is, s/he should be very careful not to generalize too broadly (beyond subjects very similar to those studied) and should be careful not to suggest sweeping changes in human affairs based on his/her research. With regard to the practical implications of any set of findings, most researchers take the position that without substantial replication no finding warrants application. It is the researcher's task, however, to think through and communicate what applications could be derived from a set of findings, should they hold up in replication.

The Decision.

The final phase of the oral examination occurs when the examination committee and dissertation committee determine whether or not the candidate has passed the oral examination. This decision is made on the basis of the quality of the project, the written document describing the project, and the oral defense of the project.

Although specific procedures differ from university to university, the candidate and all visitors are usually asked to leave the examination room prior to the deliberations and the vote. The rationale for keeping the deliberations private is clear—it is a protection of the rights of privacy of the candidate. It also probably allows the assembled committee members to be more open in their praise and criticism of the candidate. There may be another less obvious reason, also. The outcome of the decision reflects not only on the candidate, but also on his/her sponsoring committee, for they have worked with the candidate throughout the project. Thus, the criticisms by an examining committee may be considered by the dissertation committee as criticisms of its performance. The privacy of the deliberation process, then, protects the dissertation committee from a public airing of these criticisms.

After a general discussion of the candidate's project and oral performance, a vote is taken. Members of both the sponsoring committee and examining committee take part in this decision. It is expected that the group present will be able to come to a concensus, so if the initial vote results in one or more dissenting votes, discussion resumes until concensus is reached.

The faculty is not required to return a simple pass-or-fail decision, but it may suggest minor or major modifications of a project or the writing of a project in the context of either a pass-or-fail vote. In cases of minor revisions, a general practice is to pass the candidate on a conditional basis, pending the revisions requested. Usually, the examining committee delegates to the chairperson of the sponsoring committee the authority to see that the changes are made in the direction suggested. In cases of major revisions, the examining committee may choose to postpone a decision, then reconvene and conduct another oral defense. Since a number of faculty members will have read the dissertation in preparing for the oral defense, it is likely that typographical, grammatical, or other minor errors will be found in the document. Therefore, minor revisions of this nature are frequent.

Immediately after the vote is taken, the candidate is informed of the decision. If the vote is positive, from that moment on the candidate is considered to be a holder of the degree that s/he was pursuing, for all practical purposes. That is, for purposes of employment, salary, etc., s/he is said to hold the degree even if the graduation ceremony will not be held for some months.

PREPARING FOR THE EXAMINATION

At least three steps should be taken in order to insure an adequate preparation for an oral defense. First, the candidate must be sure that s/he has recently read the dissertation from cover to cover a few times. This advice seems so obvious that it seems unnecessary to mention it, but in the author's experience several students have had uncomfortable experiences, if not complete failures because they have not taken this step. It is necessary to review the project because the proposal may have been written years prior to the oral defense. Issues, such as the rationale for the project, may become somewhat fuzzy during the period in which the data collection and statistical analysis is the major preoccupation. In particular, names of key references slip from memory without review.

In reviewing the project, particular note should also be taken of ways in which the number of subjects, subject selection, data analysis, or other procedures may have changed from those discussed in the written proposal. Practical considerations often demand such changes. However, the details of the rationale for such changes may have slipped from immediate recall and may not be discussed in detail in the dissertation. It is, however, the manner in which such decisions were made that may interest an examining committee, for the evaluation is made as much on the competence of the candidate to make decisions consistent with sound research practice as on the final product.

A second method of preparation for an oral defense is to practice responding orally to questions about the research project similar to those that will be asked by the examining committee. This can be done with other students or individually. Some chairpersons of sponsoring committees or other faculty members will be willing to participate in such a practice examination. Regardless of how such practice is provided, the practice of orally defending research is beneficial because it is rare for a candidate to have had much practice of this type in his/her previous educational experiences.

A final method of preparing for an oral defense is to attend a defense in your department or in a related department. Many of the catastrophic fantasies of students about such examinations are neutralized when they see what actually occurs. Despite its obvious utility, this is the step least frequently taken by students in preparing for their defense. This is surprising, considering the option is available at most universities and the strength of student anxiety about such examinations is so great. In the author's experience, however, the students who have availed themselves of this opportunity have felt more confident as they approached their own examination.

NOTES ON FACULTY BEHAVIOR DURING THE ORAL DEFENSE

At the time of their oral defense, some students find themselves in a social situation that is quite different from what they expected it to be. One of the members of the sponsoring committee may seem to be answering the questions for the student, or two committee members may carry on a lengthy debate about some point of the research scarcely acknowledging the presence of the student. Some students find the tone of the questions asked more serious and negative than they expected, and others find that a minor point takes up most of the time of the defense because it relates to the research of one of the faculty members present who proceeds to describe his/her research in detail. Without a clear understanding of the motives and behavior of faculty members in such circumstances, a candidate may be confused by the proceedings and thus not perform as well as s/he might.

Most academic professionals go into teaching and research thinking that their working lives will be filled with reading, thought, and debate on the important intellectual facets of their field. They find, however, that their lives are filled more with advising students, editing and grading term papers, attending endless department, college, and university committee meetings, and other such secretarial and managerial functions. Time for conversation and debate with colleagues on professionally relevant issues is particularly rare. The dissertation oral defense is, however, one such occasion. It is one of the few situations in which five or more faculty members from different departments will have studied the same document and can sit down and discuss its more interesting and important implications. Thus, the oral examination serves an important function other than the evaluation of a student's work; it provides an opportunity for the expression of scholarly opinion and for debate.

The best examinations are ones in which the student participates in the conversation and debate as a peer. In such circumstances the examination is of ideas or technique, not of a degree candidate. When the student feels confident enough to disagree with points made by those present and attempts to present contrary evidence, the process can be an enjoyable and worthwhile learning experience for all those who attend. In fact, the ability to argue well for a controversial point is considered a sign of scholarly maturity and helps convince the assembled faculty of the readiness of the student to assume the status of a colleague.

Understanding that a dissertation defense is a social situation that fosters debate brings into perspective a problem that arises for some students in this situation. Some academic professionals have a crusty, aggressive questioning style which can be upsetting to the student: "I can't believe you chose that experimental design." "Why did you study this process; it always seemed unworthy of serious consideration to me." Such questions are usually not meant as personal condemnations or an indication of inferior performance. They are best understood as being a provocation to debate. By using this type of question, all that the faculty member is asking is for a persuasive statement of the rationale for a particular research design (to continue the previous examples) or for a particular research problem. There is no one best way to design a study; what questions deserve research attention is a matter of opinion. All that can be asked of any researcher is a well-thought-out rationale that is clearly presented.

It should also be kept in mind that, to a greater or lesser extent, the faculty members who attend an oral feel some pressure to perform well before their colleagues. If an examiner had no points to make regarding the student's research project, no questions, no criticisms, it would seem as if either s/he had not read the dissertation or had so little relevant knowledge that s/he could not contribute to the discussion. For these reasons, most attending faculty will come prepared to make a point or two and will have some criticisms of the research. As long as the student realizes that all research can be criticized and is willing to listen to the points made with an open mind, s/he will take these criticisms in stride.

In closing this chapter it seems appropriate to report that, of the large number of dissertation orals the author has attended, the great majority have been a pleasant educational experience for him, and for his colleagues. He feels, though, that the student being examined profited less from the discussion than the others attending because of the anxiety associated with the examination. This is unfortunate, because in such meetings the best aspects of having community of scholars are evident. This chapter was written solely for the purpose of increasing the student's understanding of these examinations, so that this anxiety can be kept within reasonable limits. If the chapter is successful, the candidate may find his/her examination a memorable and worthwhile experience.

SUMMARY

1. Five faculty members are typically required to participate in an oral defense. They include the three members of the sponsoring committee (the committee the candidate has worked with throughout the project) and two additional faculty members, who constitute the examining committee. However, other faculty and often students are allowed to attend.

2. One member of the examining committee is designated as the chairperson of the defense, and s/he serves as a moderator of the discussion as well as an examiner.

3. The oral defense can be divided into four parts, although the second and third parts frequently overlap: (1) introduction of candidate, (2) candidate's summary of project, (3) examiner questioning period, and (4) decision phase.

4. In order to prepare for the oral, the student should (1) read through the dissertation several times just prior to the defense, (2) have a practice oral defense in which friends or faculty question the student about the project, and (3) attend the dissertation defense of another student.

5. The student must realize that all research can be criticized. Therefore, all that is asked of him/her is to provide a rationale for his/her procedure.

6. The best examinations are those in which the

student and the assembled faculty debate theoretical, practical, and methodological issues, not ones where the student feels s/he is on the defensive.

A

C

P

R